Madagascar

Madagascar

BY TAMRA B. ORR

Enchantment of the World™
Second Series

CHILDREN'S PRESS®

An Imprint of Scholastic Inc.

Frontispiece: **Baobab trees**

Consultant: Laura Tilghman, PhD, Assistant Professor of Anthropology, Plymouth State University, Plymouth, New Hampshire
Please note: All statistics are as up-to-date as possible at the time of publication.

Book production by The Design Lab

Library of Congress Cataloging-in-Publication Data
Names: Orr, Tamra, author.
Title: Madagascar / by Tamra Orr.
Description: New York : Children's Press, [2017] | Series: Enchantment of the world |
   Includes bibliographical references and index.
Identifiers: LCCN 2016025117 | ISBN 9780531220849 (library binding)
Subjects: LCSH: Madagascar—Juvenile literature.
Classification: LCC DT469.M26 O67 2017 | DDC 969.1—dc23
LC record available at https://lccn.loc.gov/2016025117

1 2 3 4 5 6 7 8 9 10 R 26 25 24 23 22 21 20 19 18 17

Boy fishing

Contents

Left to right: **Planting rice, lemur, plowing, Tsingy de Bemaraha, Malagasy woman**

CHAPTER 1

Island at the End of the Earth

MILLIONS OF YEARS AGO, A DEEP RUMBLE BROKE the quiet of southern Africa. Predator and prey alike stopped moving. Sleeping creatures awoke. All inhabitants of the African world paused to listen. What was happening?

The rumble grew deeper and louder and bushes and trees began to shake all the way down into their deepest roots. Small cracks appeared in the ground, and creatures of every kind began to run, hop, or fly, each one searching for safety. The growl of the earth grew and grew. Fractures grew into cracks. Cracks turned into fissures. Fissures became gaps. Gaps became splits. It was a massive earthquake.

With a profound groan, the southeastern end of the African continent began to separate from the mainland. Over 45 million years, this land continued to shift and separate, slowly pulling away until it was separated by a 250-mile-wide (400-kilometer) swath of the Indian Ocean. With roars and grumbles,

Opposite: **A narrow sand bar connects two small islands off the northwest coast of Madagascar.**

Island at the End of the Earth **9**

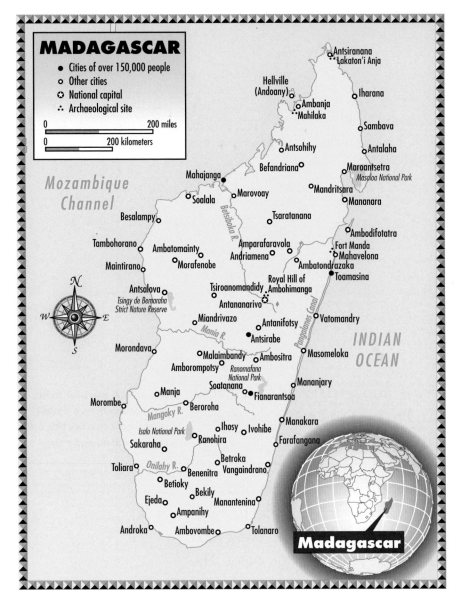

it pulled away, gently but firmly pushed by the waters of the Indian Ocean. The tip of southern Africa was now an island, an island known as Madagascar.

Remote from any other land, the plants and animals on Madagascar evolved separately from species in the rest of Africa. This means that almost all the plant and animal species on Madagascar are endemic. In other words, they are found only there.

Madagascar is one of the most isolated places in the world, earning it the nickname the Island at the End of the Earth. Experts are not sure exactly when the landmass broke off of Africa, but believe it was between 200 million and 165 million years ago. They are also not sure if an earthquake was the cause of the separation, but believe it is the best explanation.

Madagascar is the fourth-largest island in the world; only Greenland, New Guinea, and Borneo are larger. It is home to some of the most amazing animal and plant species on the planet and warm, friendly people. The first settlers on the island came not from Africa, but from across the Indian Ocean. The various groups made lives for themselves in this distant land, creating a unique culture, known as the Malagasy. Each year, hundreds of thousands of tourists arrive to see what life is like in such an unusual place. They come to watch the lemurs, smell the orchids, and get to know the people who make their home on the Island at the End of the Earth.

A wide variety of produce and other foods are for sale at markets in Madagascar.

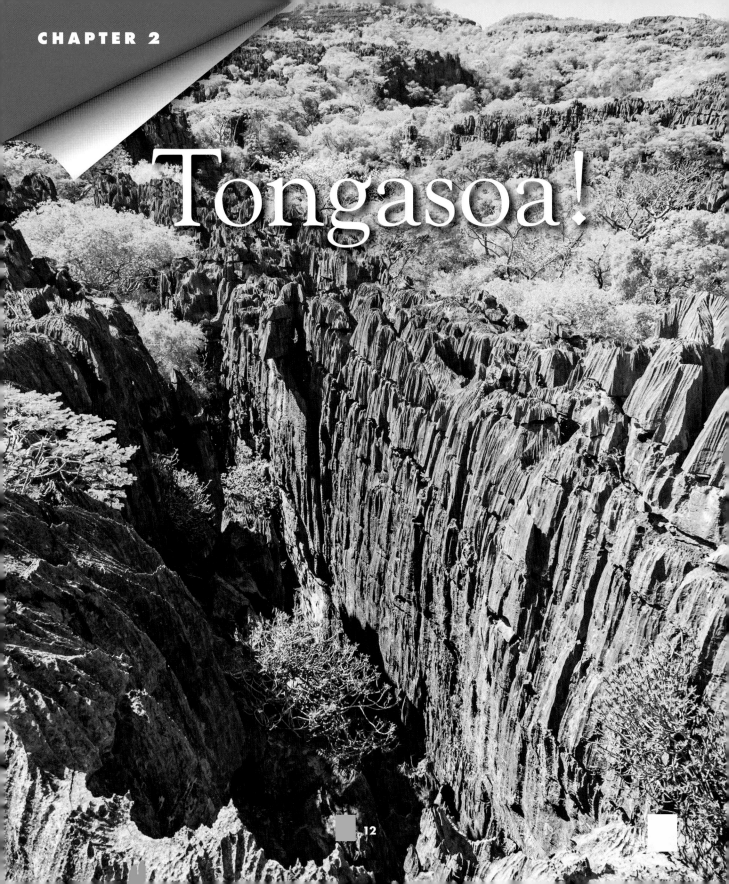

CHAPTER 2

Tongasoa!

*T*ONGASOA! WELCOME! WELCOME TO MADAGASCAR, one of the most amazing places in the world. It is a land filled with unusual plants and animals and some spectacular landscapes.

Madagascar is one of the world's largest islands. It is roughly 1,000 miles (1,600 km) long and 350 miles (560 km) wide, making it slightly larger than the U.S. state of California. It lies in the Indian Ocean off the east coast of Africa. The nearest African nation is Mozambique, and the wide stretch of water that separates Madagascar from Africa is called the Mozambique Channel.

Opposite: **Jagged limestone towers break up the land at the Tsingy de Bemaraha Strict Nature Reserve.**

Madagascar's Geographic Features

Area: 226,658 square miles (587,041 sq km)

Highest Elevation: Maromokotro, 9,436 feet (2,876 m)

Lowest Elevation: Sea level along the coast

Longest River: Mangoky, 350 miles (563 km)

Largest Lake: Alaotra, approximately 900 square miles (2,300 sq km)

Length of Coastline: 2,999 miles (4,826 km)

Highest Recorded Temperature: 97°F (36°C) in 1997

Lowest Recorded Temperature: 32°F (0°C) in 1932

Average Annual Precipitation: 39 to 59 inches (100 to 150 cm)

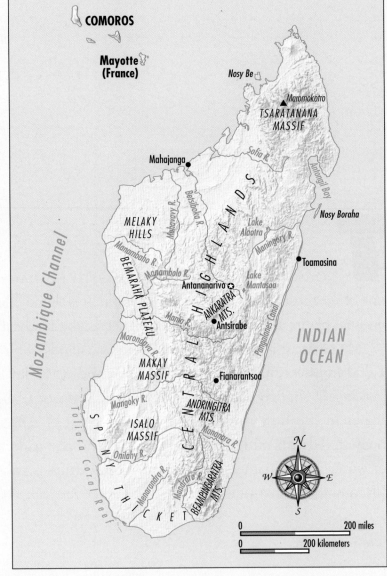

The Whale Highway: The East Coast

The east coast of Madagascar is a long, slender region, running from the Antongil Bay in the north down to the southern tip of the island. Madagascar's second-largest city, Toamasina, is found in this region. The east coast is beautiful, with sandy beaches and graceful palm and coconut trees. The east coast is sometimes called the Whale Highway, because each year migrating humpback whales gather offshore to breed.

One of the most prominent features in the east coast is the 400-mile (645 km) Pangalanes Canal. The French created it at the beginning of the twentieth century by building canals to connect rivers and lagoons. They built it for boats to have a safe place to travel, away from the rough waves of the Indian Ocean.

A man canoes down a river in northeastern Madagascar.

The rain forests of Madagascar are incredibly diverse. The forests of Masoala National Park alone contain more than 2,400 different plant species.

The east coast is the greenest region on the island, where Madagascar's rain forests are located. These lush forests are constantly wet. It is rare to have a full day go by without a period of rain. This fertile, humid area is bursting with colorful orchids, winding vines, and graceful ferns. The air is full of the sounds of wildlife, from singing birds and buzzing insects to the wails and squeaks of lemurs.

The east coast is the hottest, wettest part of Madagascar. Some places receive nearly 160 inches (400 centimeters) of rain each year. It is also the part of the country most frequently hit by the violent storms called cyclones.

Spiraling Wind

Have you ever seen a dust devil in a parking lot or playground? These happen when wind turns in a spiral. Dust devils are fascinating to watch, but what happens when they are much, much bigger and more powerful? They turn into cyclones, which are also known as hurricanes, and they are capable of enormous damage.

Madagascar has been hit by many cyclones over the years. The worst on record struck in 1994, when Cyclone Geralda landed near the eastern port city of Toamasina. It destroyed much of the city, including schools, homes, and churches. Flooding reached the capital city of Antananarivo, killing more than forty people in the process. In 2004, Cyclone Gafilo hit the island twice, with winds of more than 200 miles per hour (320 kph). It struck the island, went out to sea, changed direction, and hit a second time. The town of Antalaha was wiped out. In total, 237 people in Madagascar were killed.

In February 2012, Cyclone Giovanna struck Toamasina. It brought winds reaching 120 miles per hour (193 kph). Several people were killed, trees were ripped out of the ground, and countless homes were damaged or destroyed.

A more recent devastating cyclone was Cyclone Chedza, which hit the island in January 2015. The capital city was affected the most. Almost seventy people died in flash floods and thousands of people lost their homes and had to stay in temporary shelters.

Tsaratanana Massif: The North Region

The island's highest peak is found in the north region. Maromokotro soars to 9,436 feet (2,876 m). Maromokotro is part of an area known as Tsaratanana Massif. The word *massif* means a group of mountains that are separate from other groups. This region is hard for the rest of the people of Madagascar to reach because it is difficult to get over the mountains.

Unlike the eastern coastline, the northern coast is deeply indented. The north has several natural harbors, as well as the popular vacation island of Nosy Be to the west. This region is

Central Madagascar includes rolling hills and ancient volcanoes.

home to cities such as Antsiranana and Hellville. Many of the people who live in this region make a living by shipbuilding, tuna fishing, salt extraction, or agriculture.

A Rare Climb

Although Maromokotro is Madagascar's only high summit, few people attempt to climb it. The mountain is so remote that travelers must spend several days getting to it. According to expert mountaineer Nigel Vardy, climbers spend those days "crossing waist-deep rivers" and "bashing through dense jungle" before doing any actual climbing. Because the peak is considered sacred, climbers are expected to bring sacrifices and gifts to offer to the spirits of the ancestors. These could include chickens, money, and tobacco.

The Island's Spine: The Central Highlands

Stretching down the middle of Madagascar, from the north end of the island to the south, is the region known as the Central Highlands. It is often described as the spine of Madagascar. The elevation of the highlands ranges from 2,600 to 5,800 feet (800 to 1,770 meters). The Central Highlands feature many different types of landscapes, including smooth, rounded hills, long-extinct volcanoes, and endless rice fields.

This region has a cooler, drier climate than other parts of the island, making it better for agriculture. Madagascar's capital city of Antananarivo is in the Central Highlands, as

Women plant rice in the Central Highlands. Rice is the main crop in the region.

The Cities of Madagascar

The largest city in Madagascar is its capital, Antananarivo, with a population of 1,391,433 in 2016. The nation's second-largest city, Toamasina, lies on the east coast and is home to 206,373. Toamasina is the island's busiest port, with most of Madagascar's imports and exports moving through this city. Away from the port, the city has broad boulevards lined with palm trees, bustling markets, huge numbers of *pousse-pousses* (passenger carts pulled by people), and a university that opened in 1977.

The next largest city is Antsirabe (below), with a population of 186,253. Located in central Madagascar, it sits on one of the island's highest peaks in the Ankaratra Mountains. The city is a center of agriculture and of

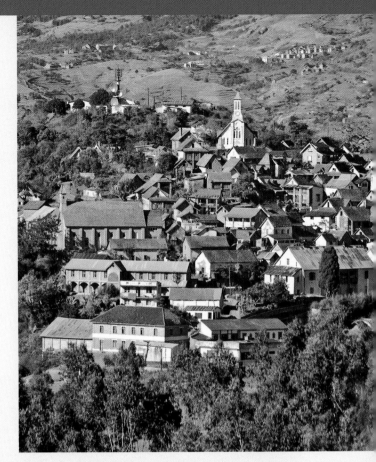

textile manufacturing. The Sabotsy (Saturday) market offers something for everyone, from colorful fabric to ripe fruit. Thanks to its high elevation and its own thermal springs, Antsirabe also has a popular health resort.

The city of Fianarantsoa (above), home to 167,227, is found in south-central Madagascar. Its name means "the place where one can learn something good," and it remains an educational and religious center. The city also boasts a beautiful old town and vibrant market.

Mahajanga, in northwestern Madagascar, has a population of 154,657. It began as a trade town between Madagascar and the Middle East. For years, businesses boomed in cattle, slaves, arms, and spices. Today, the city is home to many people of Indian descent.

are many of the nation's other large cities. They serve as the center for business and government for all of Madagascar. Additionally, the highlands are the site of several national parks and the island's largest lakes, Mantasoa and Alaotra.

Mangrove trees rise from the water near the Madagascar coast. The submerged roots of the trees create areas where baby fish and other sea life can find protection.

Harbors and Swamps: The West Coast

Madagascar's west coast has many natural harbors and has attracted explorers, traders, and pirates for many years. Along the coast are mangrove swamps edging sandy beaches. Mangrove trees are amazing trees in that they can live with their roots in salty water. The west coast is much drier than the east, and between May and November it never rains in the west at all. Madagascar's second-largest port, Mahajanga, is in this region.

Desert Land: The Southwest

The driest part of Madagascar is in the southwest region. In this part of the country, it rains only during the first three months of the year. The limited fertile areas are used to grow rice, corn, and cassava, while the rest of the land is mainly used for raising cattle.

This region features spiny forests, made up of cactus-like plants such as the prickly pear. This fruit is used to provide food and water for herds of cattle.

Isalo National Park is found in this area. It amazes visitors with its impressive rock formations, deep canyons, and crystal-clear natural pools.

A road winds through the dry landscape amid rugged rock formations at Isalo National Park.

Madagascar's Spiny Thicket

The spiny thicket is one of the most amazing places in the world, full of incredible trees and wildlife. But getting into the thicket to explore it is tricky—and sometimes painful. There is no shade, and there are lots of spiky plants to get snagged on or cut by.

The spiny thicket is part desert and part forest. It is full of bizarrely shaped trees that are found nowhere else in the world. Some of the trees do not have any branches, but instead have long, sharp spikes. Others have fat trunks and short, stubby branches. They are called elephant foot trees. Others have trunks shaped like triangles. Scientists suspect the reason these trees are all so strange is that they have had to learn how to grow in a region that often goes half a year or more without a drop of rain.

Despite their odd shapes, these trees are full of birds stopping by to perch on some branches. Several types of tortoises live in the spiny thicket, along with lemurs and mongooses.

Disappearing Trees

Long ago, Madagascar's forests were larger than they are today. But over the years, the amount of forested land on the island has steadily declined. Today, about 21 percent of Madagascar is forested.

The trees have been disappearing for many reasons. One major cause is illegal logging. The Madagascar rain forest contains ebony, rosewood, and other valuable hardwoods. Illegal loggers take these trees and sell the lumber overseas, where it is turned into furniture, musical instruments, and other expensive goods.

The forests have also been cleared so people can use the land. Some more trees are cut down for people to use as fuel for fires to heat their homes. Still more land in Madagascar has been cleared of trees to make way for rice farms, while other areas have been cleared to create pastures for cattle. These trees are often cleared by a process known as slash and burn, or *tavy*. This method can be dangerous, because the fires sometimes get out of control, destroying surrounding forests.

The loss of trees has destroyed the habitat of many of Madagascar's plants and animals. Countless species are in dan-

Nothing but stumps remain where a Madagascar forest has been cleared to make room for agriculture.

Tsingy de Bemaraha Strict Nature Reserve

The Tsingy de Bemaraha Strict Nature Reserve lies in west-central Madagascar. Anyone who visits is sure to see some amazing species of lemurs and birds—but it is not a place for the fainthearted. In fact, bravery is as necessary there as comfortable shoes.

The word *tsingy* means "where one cannot walk barefoot," and it is easy to see how this nature reserve got that name. The majority of Tsingy de Bemaraha is made up of sharp rocks and jagged limestone formations. In some places, visitors make their way over these formations on long rope bridges spanning drops of 300 feet (90 m) or more. Crossing the bridges may be frightening, but they provide a remarkable view of this incredible stone forest.

ger of dying out because they are losing their homes and their food sources. Hundreds of species are endangered.

There is hope, however. The island's government, as well as foreign donors and international organizations, has been pumping millions of dollars into protecting Madagascar's environment. The government has promised to dedicate thousands of acres to reforestation. It is also working to set up six types of protected areas: strict nature reserves, special nature reserves, national parks, conservation sites, classified forests, and reforestation zones. Hopefully, these efforts will help protect the creatures and plants of Madagascar before it is too late.

CHAPTER 3

Land of the Lemurs

MADAGASCAR HAS SOME OF THE MOST AMAZING plants and animals found anywhere on the planet. Thanks to its isolation from the rest of the world, animal and plant species have been able to grow and develop with little interference. An incredible 85 percent of the wildlife on Madagascar is found only on this island. That's the good news. The bad news, however, is that many of these species are in danger of becoming extinct. As people have used the land, the animals' habitats have been broken up or destroyed.

Opposite: **The crowned lemur spends much of its time high in the trees, but it descends to the ground sometimes to pick up fruit, find fruit, or move to a new area.**

There are many stories told of mythical animals that roam the island of Madagascar. The *fanany* is a snake with seven horned heads. The *songomby* is an ox that feasts on people, while the *lalomena* is another ox that has bright red horns and lives in the water.

Scariest of all, in the island's tall tales, are the *kalanoro*. They are people who live in the hills of the deep forest and have long beards, bright eyes, and feet that point backward. They are said to have magical power and supernatural strength.

Mammals

No animal is more associated with Madagascar than lemurs, small primates with a wide-eyed stare. It is believed that lemurs first arrived in Madagascar from Africa on tangled mats of plants more than sixty million years ago. At the time, Madagascar was home to no mammals or birds, so the lemurs had no predators to worry about. They grew, changed, and thrived. Back in Africa, the original lemur species died out. But in Madagascar, more than one hundred types of lemurs developed across the island. Today, most lemur species are in danger of becoming extinct. Their numbers have dropped as they have been hunted and forests have been cut down, destroying their habitat.

Many other unique animals are also found only in Madagascar. The fossa looks like a cross between a cat and a dog, but is actually related to the mongoose. The fossa is the

A fossa rests in a tree in Madagascar.

Wandering Spirits

The word *lemur* means "wandering spirit," and these creatures do move about, often jumping from tree to tree as if they have wings. The lemurs in Madagascar vary tremendously. They range from the tiny mouse lemur that fits in the palm of a person's hand to the large indri lemur that stands several feet tall.

The aye-aye species looks like a mix of animals, with teeth like a beaver's, eyes like a bat's, and a tail like a fox's. This lemur comes out only at night. It has a bony middle finger that it uses to tap trees while it listens for the movement of tasty insect larvae inside.

The sifaka lemur (left) is delightful to watch. It moves around by dancing and leaping on its back legs, arms up over its head. The indri lemur communicates by calling out loudly from trees. Its vocalizations sound much like the underwater calls of a humpback whale.

The ring-tailed lemur (above) gets its name from its long, black-and-white striped tail. Like most lemurs, it lives in family clusters run by females.

The Giant Jumping Rat

The largest rodent found in Madagascar is the giant jumping rat. It is about the same size as the average rabbit and even looks like one. It has long, pointy ears, short fur, and large rear feet designed for—as its name says—jumping. When threatened by a predator such as a fossa, the rat can jump 3 feet (1 m) straight up in the air. The giant jumping rat lives in burrows and comes out at night to seek fruit and seeds.

island's largest predator, reaching as long as 6.5 feet (2 m) from the tip of its snout to the tip of its tail. Fossas hunt for food at night and enjoy snacking on lemurs, birds, and reptiles. They use their tails to help them balance as they move from one branch to the next.

Another of Madagascar's unusual creatures is the tenrec. It lives in the forests of western Madagascar. The tenrec is a small animal that looks similar to a hedgehog. The island has several species of tenrecs, but one of the oddest is the aquatic tenrec. It lives on land but is adapted for the water, with strong back legs and webbed feet. Aquatic tenrecs search the bottom of shallow water, using their whiskers to locate fish and tadpoles. Once they find a meal, they bring it to the surface and then roll on their backs in order to kill the prey by kicking it to death.

Amphibians, Reptiles, and Birds

The only amphibians in Madagascar are frogs, but there are a lot of them—more than three hundred species. One of the

most unusual frogs is the tomato frog. It gets its name from the bright red color of the female. Tomato frogs live in the northern part of the island. They live on insects but won't turn down anything small enough to fit into their mouths. Like some toads, if they are threatened, tomato frogs secrete a poisonous chemical that sends predators scurrying away after one lick.

Madagascar is home to hundreds of snakes. One of the oddest is the Malagasy leaf-nosed snake. These snakes have unusual noses that look like leaves. This helps them hide in trees and capture tasty lizards for lunch.

Many lizards are found on the island, including more than 150 chameleons. Like other chameleons, the panther chameleon changes color based on its mood. What makes this

Female tomato frogs are often bright red. Males are usually browner in tone.

A panther chameleon's tongue is often longer than its body.

chameleon unusual is that it can rotate and focus its two eyes independently of each other. This means the panther chameleon can look at two separate things at the same time. When it comes time to attack prey, however, it focuses both eyes on its target and then launches its long, sticky tongue. Gulp! It's dinnertime.

Hundreds of species of birds are found in Madagascar. The subdesert mesite is an odd bird because it refuses to fly, even when it is threatened. Instead, it freezes in hopes that its dull coloring will help it blend in with its surroundings and it will become invisible. The mesite uses it wings only to fly to its nest up in the trees.

The Ancient Elephant Bird

Long ago, Madagascar was home to one of the largest flightless birds in history. Known as the elephant bird, it weighed more than 1,100 pounds (500 kilograms) and stood 10 feet (3 m) tall. It was related to today's ostriches and emus. The elephant bird had huge legs, sharp claws, and a long, strong neck. Although it had a spear-like beak, it was a plant eater.

The elephant bird has been extinct since the seventeenth century, due to both hunting and habitat loss. Museums in Madagascar display elephant bird eggs that have been preserved. They weigh as much as 20 pounds (9 kg). Experts say that one egg would have been enough to make an omelet capable of feeding 150 people!

Island Insects

Tens of thousands of insect species live on Madagascar. One of the most unusual is the comet, or moon, moth. This is one of the biggest moths in the world. Its wings can span 8 inches (20 cm), and its long tail often adds another 6 inches (15 cm). Once they are fully grown, comet moths live less than a week, but during that time, they lay up to 170 eggs.

Another odd insect, the giraffe-necked weevil, is found in the eastern wet forests of this country. Like its name implies, this insect has a very, very long neck, often two to three times the length of the rest of its red and black body. When two males battle over a female weevil, the one with the longer neck is usually the winner.

Cockroaches are found all over the world, but the ones in Madagascar are different. The Madagascar hissing cockroaches

An Unwelcome Creature

Some insects found in Madagascar are helpful, and some are annoying. And there is one that is particularly destructive: the locust. Locusts are a type of grasshopper that eat nonstop. During many years, there are few of them, but during other years they multiply in numbers and gather into huge swarms. In 2012, Madagascar was infested with these insects. The locust swarms continued for years, resulting in a state of emergency throughout the island. Billions of the buzzing insects filled the air, flying in clusters miles wide. "It's like you are in a movie, it's incredible," said Alexandre Huynh of the Food and Agriculture Organization of the United Nations. "You don't see anything except locusts. You turn around, there are locusts everywhere." The locust swarms do not directly hurt humans, but they cause devastation by devouring crops needed to feed the country's people and cattle. The Madagascar government has rallied to protect its people by spraying millions of acres with pesticides to kill the bugs. The

Food and Agriculture Organization of the United Nations hopes to set up an early warning system so that, at the very first sign of locusts, preventive measures can be taken. In the meantime, the fight between humans and insects continues.

are brown, oval-shaped, and have no wings. The males are easy to spot because they have large horns on their heads. They use these horns like deer use antlers, ramming them at other insects to fight for food or mates. But listen! These insects are named hissing cockroaches for a reason. As they battle, the insects make a loud hissing sound. Unlike other noisemaking insects like crickets, the cockroaches do not rub body parts together or vibrate to make a sound. Instead, they quickly exhale air through a row of breathing holes, called spiracles, on their abdomen. The action is similar to what humans do when they

sigh, but for these insects, it creates a hiss. Madagascar hissing cockroaches live on the forest floor, hiding under logs, leaves, and dirt during the day and then coming out at night to look for fruit or leaves to munch. They hiss only to sound an alarm or when they battle other cockroaches.

Of the nine species of baobab in the world, six are endemic to Madagascar. The largest of these, Grandidier's baobab, can grow as much as 100 feet (30 m) tall.

Plant Life

Nearly fourteen thousand plant species are found on the island of Madagascar, and three-quarters of them are endemic. Madagascar has more than 160 species of palm trees alone. One of the most unusual types of trees found on the island is the baobab. At first glance, these trees look like they have somehow grown upside down, with the roots up in the air, reaching for the sun. In fact, one of Madagascar's oldest folk stories is that these trees were created by the devil, who, in a

Personality of the Century

Albert Rakoto Ratsimamanga (1907–2001) was one of Madagascar's most beloved scientists. He spent years studying the endemic flowers of the island and researching how they could be used to help in medicine. He wrote more than 350 scientific papers on natural treatments for health problems, ranging from cancer to diabetes. He was quoted as saying, "We need to proceed at our own pace, we need to trust ourselves and the healing virtues of nature. In the end, nature and man are nothing but one and the same entity."

In addition to studying plants, Ratsimamanga was active in politics and was the cofounder of the Association of Malagasy Students, a group that fought against France's control of the island. He had several honorary degrees in medical research, and local television viewers elected him "Personality of the Century."

fury, turned over random trees. Baobabs are actually a type of succulent plant, like some types of cacti or aloe plants. They store their water in their thick trunks, and thirsty people know they can get a much-needed drink from one of these trees. Traditionally, some people in Madagascar used the baobab's bark for making clothes, baskets, and canoes. Today, the sweet and tangy fruit of the baobab remains popular on the island.

Madagascar is also home to the flower the rosy periwinkle. At first glance, this bright pink flower may not seem like anything unusual, but it has given the world two cancer-fighting drugs used to treat leukemia and Hodgkin's disease. The island features almost a thousand species of orchids, including a unique five-star

flower known as Darwin's orchid, named for Charles Darwin, who developed the theory of evolution.

Toliara Coral Reef

Off the southwestern coast of Madagascar is the Toliara coral reef, the third-largest coral reef system in the world. Hundreds of different species live in and around the coral reef, including sea turtles and the coelacanth, a rare fish. The coelacanth was thought to be extinct until a live specimen was caught in 1938. The coelacanth is a huge fish, as long as 6.5 feet (2 m), and tends to live in the deepest and darkest of waters.

Unfortunately, climate change is endangering the coral reef. As the earth's temperature rises, sea temperatures also rise. This alters the chemistry of the ocean, which can kill the coral.

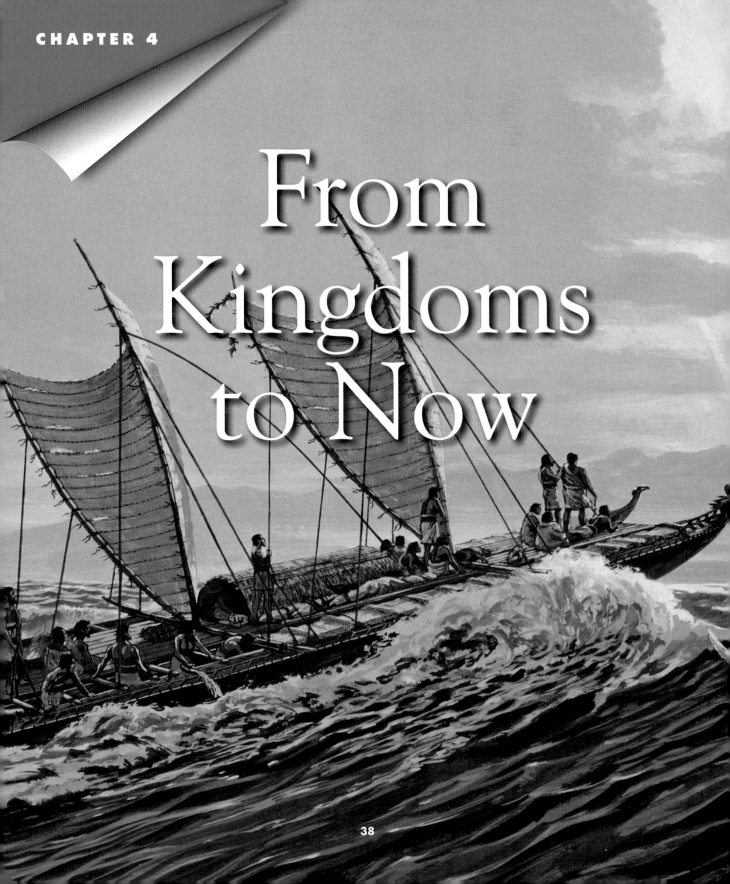

CHAPTER 4

From Kingdoms to Now

WHEN THE ISLAND OF MADAGASCAR SEPARATED from Africa millions of years ago, there were no people on earth yet. Although modern humans evolved about two hundred thousand years ago, people reached the island of Madagascar perhaps two thousand years ago. Experts are not certain who arrived there first. Some believe the first inhabitants were from islands in Southeast Asia that are now part of Indonesia, thousands of miles to the east. They crossed the Indian Ocean in outrigger canoes. Others might have arrived from India, Africa, and the Middle East. A genetic study of the people of Madagascar has indicated that at least half of them are descended from the people of Borneo, a large island 4,500 miles (7,200 km) away that is split between Indonesia, Malaysia, and Brunei.

Opposite: **The first people came to Madagascar in canoes.**

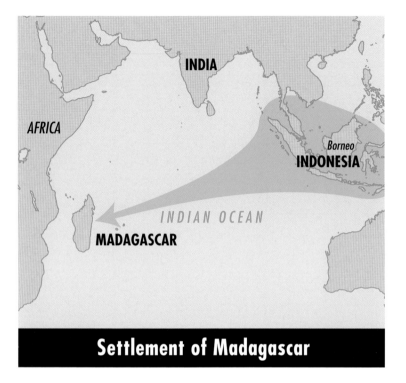

Settlement of Madagascar

Early Settlers

The earliest evidence of human settlement in Madagascar discovered to date is a rock shelter on the coast near what is now Antsiranana, in the northern part of the country. The site is called Lakaton'i Anja, and it dates to about 420 CE. Researchers have found bits of pottery along with the remains of animals there.

Until about 1000 CE, most settlements in Madagascar were on the coast. By this time, people had started to engage in trade, and Dutch beads and Chinese pottery have been discovered at some sites. In particular, the island of Nosy Mangabe was an important center of trade. There is also evidence that people in Madagascar were working with iron.

After 1000 CE, some people began moving inland, where they grew rice and kept livestock. Meanwhile, some of the settlements along the coast became cities. Mahilaka, in the northwest, became an important port and the center of a group of villages. Some parts of the Mahilaka region produced glass or iron. Others were dedicated to agriculture. Mahilaka was surrounded by walls 8 feet (2.5 m) high and 20 feet (6 m) thick. Experts estimate that at its height, Mahilaka was home

An Unexpected Discovery

Portuguese navigator Diogo Dias stumbled across Madagascar by accident. He and his brother Bartolomeu had been on an expedition to India with Pedro Álvares Cabral when his ship was blown off course at the Cape of Good Hope at the southern tip of Africa. Dias lost sight of the rest of the fleet of ships.

On August 10, 1500, he and his men spotted Madagascar, becoming the first Europeans to set eyes on the island. Dias named it St. Lawrence, and then turned his ship around and headed back to Portugal. Bartolomeu Dias did not fare as well. His ship hit a storm and everyone aboard was lost at sea.

to between 3,500 and 17,500 people. Then, suddenly, in the fourteenth or fifteenth century, Mahilaka was abandoned. This may have been because of the bubonic plague, or Black Death, that swept the world during this time.

By the 1500s, settlements in Madagascar typically consisted of a town with five to ten connected villages in the surrounding area. People raised food, made crafts, and imported goods. Over time, chiefs or kings emerged in these settlements.

The Arrival of Europeans

During the seventh century, Arabs came to Madagascar and set up trading posts along the northwest coast. It was not until Portuguese explorer Diogo Dias lost his way and spotted Madagascar in 1500 that Europeans found out about the island. The Dutch came to Madagascar, followed by the French, Portuguese, and English. All of them tried to set up

The Sakalava people lived in the west of Madagascar. They formed the island's first major kingdom.

trading settlements on the island, but the people already there fought back and scared them away. Since the Europeans had found no evidence of valuable goods such as ivory, gold, or spices, they saw no reason to stay.

In 1642, France tried once again to set up a colony on Madagascar, but between the hostility of the inhabitants, constant exposure to diseases, and frequent visits from pirates, the French gave up on this attempt.

The Kingdoms of Madagascar

When Europeans began to show interest in Madagascar, the island was home to several large groups called kingdoms. The western and northern parts of the island were ruled by the Sakalava people. The Central Highlands were largely controlled by a group known as the Merina. They were first led by King Andrianampoinimerina. By trading with the Europeans, the Merina had acquired a large supply of weapons. They used these weapons to expand their control across Madagascar, including areas that had been held by Sakalava groups to the west. In 1800, the royalty moved to the new capital city, Antananarivo.

Under King Andrianampoinimerina, the Merina people gained control of much of the Central Highlands.

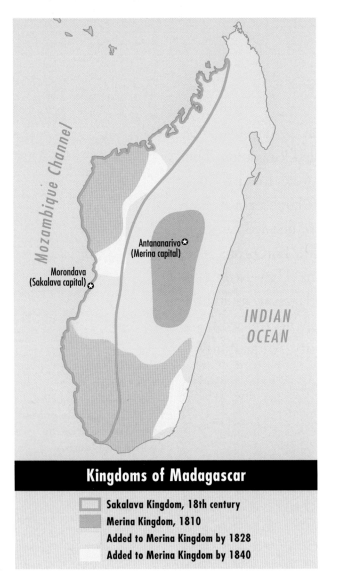

Kingdoms of Madagascar

☐ Sakalava Kingdom, 18th century
■ Merina Kingdom, 1810
■ Added to Merina Kingdom by 1828
☐ Added to Merina Kingdom by 1840

When King Andrianampoinimerina died in 1810, his role was given to his eighteen-year-old son, Radama I. The new king increased the island's army to thirty-five thousand men. To help unite people, the king put a Frenchman in charge of his army and hired an Englishman to be his personal adviser. In 1817, Radama I and the British government came to an agreement that Madagascar was an independent state under Merina control.

Life changed a great deal for the Malagasy, the people of Madagascar, after this agreeement. European missionaries came in to convert people to Christianity, a Latin alphabet was created to represent the language, and the Malagasy were taught skills such as weaving, woodworking, and blacksmithing. In addition, Radama's army gained uniforms, additional arms, and more training.

Wicked Queens

Radama I died in 1828 and his wife, Queen Ranavalona, took over. Known in history as "the wicked queen," she was not a popular ruler. She immediately made Christianity illegal and exiled or executed any of the missionaries left in the region.

The Ghosts at Île Sainte Marie

Just off the east coast of Madagascar is the island of Sainte Marie, known to the Malagasy as Nosy Boraha. During the seventeenth and eighteenth centuries, pirates from England, Portugal, France, and the Americas came to plunder the ships returning from Asia laden with silk, spices, and other precious goods. Today, tourists can still see the wrecks of some pirate ships in the shallow waters of the bay. Some experts believe these are the remains of Captain Kidd's *Adventure Galley* and Captain Condent's *Fiery Dragon*. Visitors can also visit the graves of these men in the pirates' cemetery. Any tombstone with a skull and swords marks the grave of a pirate. Today, the island is full of hotels and resorts—and perhaps the ghosts of long forgotten pirates.

In the 1800s, many European missionaries traveled to Madagascar to try to convert the Malagasy to Christianity. Some Malagasy then became ministers.

A Merina Fort

At the beginning of the nineteenth century, King Radama I ordered a fort to be built northeast of the coastal town Mahavelona, north of Taomasina. He wanted to use it to defend the island against any foreign invaders who approached the east coast. It took eight years to complete Fort Manda. The walls were 26 feet (8 m) tall and, in some parts, 20 feet (6 m) thick. They were made from a mix of coral, sand, and eggshells. To cement these ingredients in place, the Malagasy used more than 150,000 egg whites.

The fort was home to Governor Rafaralahy, the man in charge of the royal army. Inside the circular fort were barracks and houses for up to twenty-five thousand soldiers and officers, as well as an arsenal and a prison.

In 1898, the French overpowered the men at Fort Manda. Many of the Merina people used a secret tunnel to escape. Later, the fort was used as a place for villagers, pirates, and thieves to hide. Today, visitors can tour the fort and see some of its original cannons and barracks walls. Although the Merina people built five similar forts, only Manda still stands today.

All foreigners were forced to leave and anyone who dared to challenge her was assassinated. She even ordered the deaths of any babies born on what she determined was an "unlucky day." Many people rebelled, but to no avail. When she died in 1861, people were relieved. The throne was taken over by her son, Radama II.

As a strong believer in the freedom of religion, Radama II worked to reinstate Christianity as the official religion of Madagascar. He invited Europeans back to the island. Before he could make very many changes, however, he was murdered by his wife, Rasoherina, and other royal staff.

For the next thirty years, Madagascar was technically ruled by a queen, first Rasoherina, then Ranavalona II, followed by Ranavalona III. Each of the three queens married the same man, the country's prime minister, Rainilaiarivony, and he was truly in control.

Rainilaiarivony wanted to modernize the country. He set up a more organized government, established a code of laws, and made education compulsory. He also worked to suppress traditional religion.

Prime Minister Rainilaiarivony (left) and his wife, Queen Ranavalona III. Ranavalona served as queen from 1883 to 1897.

Inside the Queen's Palace

On the highest hill in the city of Antananarivo sits the Queen's Palace, also named Manjakamiadana, which means "a fine place to rule." The palace was designed in the mid-1800s for Queen Ranavalona I by an architect named James Cameron. The palace gate has a huge carved eagle in mid-flight above it. This was a symbol of military power.

In 1995, a massive fire swept through the palace, destroying much of it, and it is still being rebuilt. The grounds are littered with other ruins, the result of a succession of rulers who destroyed whatever buildings were there before they took control.

Near the Queen's Palace is the Andafiavaratra Palace. It is a museum that contains many of the artifacts that survived the 1995 fire. Several tombs are near the palace. Gray tombstones indicate the graves of kings, while red ones were used for queens. Many tourists come to the Queen's Palace, but it is important for them to remember that it is forbidden to point their fingers directly at the tombs or the palace.

Under French Control

France was still determined to take control of Madagascar, and it fought hard to get it. The French were interested in Madagascar because it was important strategically. At the time, India was a valuable British colony, and to reach India, ships passed by Madagascar.

In 1883, a French warship arrived just off the coast of Toamasina. Cannons bombarded the city, and then troops attacked. Years of fighting followed. Finally, France won, and in 1896, it took over all of Madagascar. French became the official language, and all Merina royalty was abolished.

The Royal Hill of Ambohimanga

The Royal Hill of Ambohimanga, just outside the capital city of Antananarivo, is considered one of the island's most sacred spots. The island's Merina royalty once lived here, and the site features ruins that date back five hundred years. The king's home, made out of solid rosewood, still stands. The wall surrounding the village is built of rock kept in place with mortar made from a combination of egg whites and lime juice. Artifacts found on the site include the king's drums and weapons. Burial sites are scattered throughout the area and the Malagasy still consider it a place of worship.

The queen and prime minister were sent to Algeria in North Africa. Railroads were built and roads were improved. Soon forests were being cut down en masse to make room for sugarcane, cotton, and coffee plantations.

Independence at Last

The people of Madagascar continually fought for their country's freedom from France. As many as one hundred thousand Malagasy died in during a rebellion in the early twentieth century. In 1947, a group known as the Democratic Movement for Malagasy Renewal battled the French army, but lost as many as eighty thousand people in the uprising.

In 1956, the French passed the Overseas Reform Act, giving its colonies greater freedom. This act gave all Malagasy the right to vote. It also allowed the local assembly in Madagascar to elect a leader for the region. In the following years, Madagascar continued moving toward independence,

Rebels surrender after the 1947 Malagasy uprising against the French.

and in 1960, it became fully independent from France. The people of Madagascar elected a president and looked to the future with hope.

Time of Turmoil

Although Madagascar finally had independence, its troubles were not over. The next few decades were filled with strikes, protests, violence, and a constant change in leadership.

In 1959, the people elected their first president, Philibert Tsiranana. He maintained close ties with France. Some people did not approve of this, and resentment grew. In 1972, shortly after being reelected, Tsiranana was forced to resign.

That year, General Gabriel Ramanantsoa assumed the

position of prime minister. For several years, the island was under martial law, meaning that the army had control over the people and the laws governing them. Under Ramanantsoa, Madagascar's relationship with France became much cooler. French military forces left the island, and the nation began getting military support from the Soviet Union, a large communist nation in eastern Europe and western Asia.

In 1975, Colonel Didier Ratsiraka was named Madagascar's new president. The country was renamed the Democratic Republic of Madagascar. Under Ratsiraka, some banks and

French president Charles de Gaulle shakes hands with Philibert Tsiranana, the first president of Madagascar, in 1959.

industries were taken over by the government. It was a difficult time economically, and poverty worsened. When Ratsiraka was reelected for a second term in 1982, and then a third in 1989, riots broke out among the people who suspected the election had been rigged for Ratsiraka to win. Many people went on strike, and at one point, half a million Malagasy demonstrated outside the presidential palace. A number of them were shot and killed. Finally, in late 1991, Ratsiraka agreed to share his political power with Albert Zafy, the opposition leader.

Didier Ratsiraka was the leader of Madagascar for more than twenty years.

Albert Zafy casts his vote during the 1992 election.

In 1992, a new constitution was written, and Madagascar was renamed the Republic of Madagascar. The constitution identified the island as a state with multiple political parties, and limited the amount of power given to the president. Power shifted to Zafy and then back to Ratsiraka. In 1998, Ratsiraka changed the country's constitution, giving more power to the president and allowing him to abolish the parliament if he so chose.

By the time of the elections in 2001, the people of Madagascar were more than ready to see someone defeat Ratsiraka. The main opponent was Marc Ravalomanana, the

A Defender of the Innocent

Gisèle Rabesahala spent her entire life working to help others. She was born in 1929 and spent much of her young life moving around, because her father was an officer in the French army. When her father died in 1942, she returned to her homeland of Madagascar. Even as a small child, Rabesahala knew she wanted to help others and to be a "defender of the innocent." By the time she was seventeen, she was involved in politics and working as secretary to the Democratic Movement for Malagasy Renewal, which fought for Madagascar's independence.

She pushed hard for her country's independence. In 1956, she became a city council representative in Antananarivo, making her the first woman in the country elected to a political position. She was also the first Malagasy woman to lead a political party, in 1958, and to be appointed a minister in the government, in 1977.

Rabesahala dedicated her life to the freedom of her people, as well as the need for basic human rights. She died in 2011.

mayor of Antananarivo. After the votes were in, Ratsiraka looked like he had won again, but there were great protests that the politician had rigged the votes. For six months, the island was in a state of limbo amid arguments over who won the election. Finally, Ravalomanana declared himself the winner. As a result, Ratsiraka declared martial law and blocked food and fuel from being delivered to Antananarivo. At the same time, he attempted to establish himself as president, based in the city of Toamasina.

Finally, an official recount was done and the high constitutional court declared Ravalomanana the official winner. Ratsiraka at last left the country and the crisis came to an end.

Under Ravalomanana's rule, the island's economy improved, and the president focused on developing partnerships with other countries and supporting the environment. Ravalomanana was elected to a second term in 2006. By 2009, he had forcibly closed television and radio programs produced by his political opponent Andry Rajoelina, inciting protests. Many of the protesters were killed in antigovernment demonstrations and the country's parliament was shut down.

In March, Ravalomanana resigned and was exiled to South Africa. Once more the island was under military rule. Military leaders named Rajoelina president. People around the world were disappointed at Madagascar's lack of democratic progress.

In 2014, former finance minister Hery Rajaonarimampianina was elected president. By the end of 2015, the Senate had been put back into place, six years after it had been dissolved. Rajaonarimampianina hopes to find ways to help Madagascar's fragile economy.

Protesters face soldiers on the streets of Antananarivo during the political crisis of 2009.

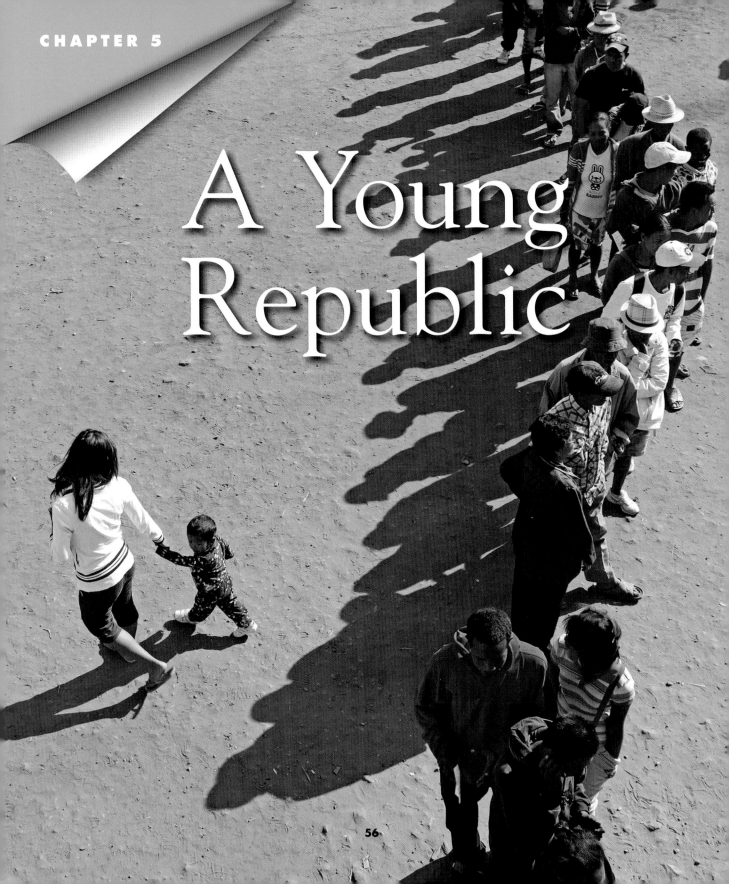

CHAPTER 5

A Young Republic

SINCE BECOMING INDEPENDENT, MADAGASCAR has struggled to maintain its democracy. Leaders have been forced out, and the parliament was shut down for several years. But in recent years, a new president was elected, and parliament was reopened. People hope that the nation's fragile democracy will continue to strengthen.

Opposite: **People stand in line waiting to vote in Antananarivo.**

Seeing Red

The color red has great meaning for the people of Madagascar. The country is sometimes referred to as the Red Island, because of the color of much of its soil. In the seventeenth century, the Sakalava people called their land Menabe, which means "great red." When the Merina people came into power, they added white to the red for their country's colors.

When Madagascar moved toward independence in the mid-twentieth century, it wanted a new flag. It kept the red and white colors from earlier times, and added green. The colors stand for purity (white), sovereignty (red), and hope (green). This flag was formally adopted on October 14, 1958.

Malagasy people gather at a political rally.

Structure of Government

Madagascar's government is organized according to its most recent constitution, which was written in 2010. The constitution established Madagascar as a multiparty republic. A republic is a form of government in which people elect representatives who serve as their voice in government, and the head of state is a president rather than a king or queen.

Like other countries around the world, Madagascar's government has three branches. They are the executive, the legislative, and the judicial.

Madagascar's National Government

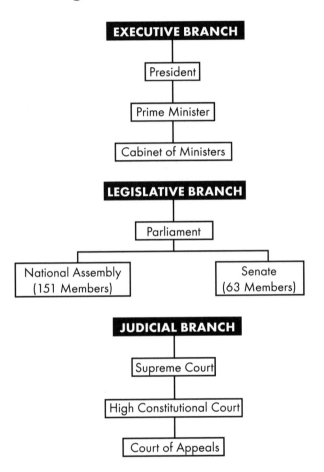

EXECUTIVE BRANCH
- President
- Prime Minister
- Cabinet of Ministers

LEGISLATIVE BRANCH
- Parliament
  - National Assembly (151 Members)
  - Senate (63 Members)

JUDICIAL BRANCH
- Supreme Court
- High Constitutional Court
- Court of Appeals

Executive Branch

The head of the executive branch of government is the president, who is elected by the people to a five-year term. In Madagascar, everyone who is at least eighteen years old can vote.

The president appoints the prime minister, who is in charge of managing the government. The prime minister is

President Hery Rajaonarimampianina was born outside Antananarivo in 1958. He earned a master's degree in business administration in Madagascar, and then moved to Canada to study accounting and finance. After returning to his homeland in 1991, Rajaonarimampianina opened a nationwide accounting firm.

In 2009, Rajaonarimampianina was named Minister of Finance and Budget. He won the presidency in 2014 in a race that involved thirty-two other candidates.

Hery Rajaonarimampianina has the longest name of any head of state in the world. According to experts, his name should be pronounced "HAIR Rah-djaw-nah-ri-mam-pee-ah-nee-EN."

generally the head of the largest party or coalition (group of parties working together) in the parliament.

The prime minister is advised by a cabinet of ministers who are in charge of different policy areas. For example, Madagascar has a minister of economy and planning, a minister of national education, and a minister of trade and consumer affairs.

Legislative Branch

Madagascar's lawmaking body, or parliament, has two houses: the National Assembly and the Senate. The number of members in each of these bodies has changed several times. In 2016, the National Assembly had 151 members and the Senate had 63 members.

The members of the National Assembly are elected by the people to five-year terms. The members of the Senate are

chosen in two different ways. Forty-two of them are elected by local mayors and councillors. The other twenty-one senators are appointed by the president.

Ban Ki-moon, the leader of the United Nations, speaks to a joint session of the Senate and National Assembly of Madagascar in 2016.

Judicial Branch

Madagascar's judicial branch of government is based on the French system. Its higher courts include the Supreme Court, the High Constitutional Court, and the Court of Appeals.

The Supreme Court has eleven members who are elected by the president and judicial officials to three-year terms. The Supreme Court does not deal with common criminal or civil court cases. Instead, it handles only issues of judicial administration.

In Malagasay, the name of Madagascar's national anthem is "Ry Tanindrazanay malala ô!" This translates to "Oh, Our Beloved Fatherland." The lyrics were written by Pasteur Rahajason, and the music is by Norbert Raharisoa. It was adopted as Madagascar's official national anthem in 1959.

Malagasy lyrics

Ry Tanindrazanay malala ô!
Ry Madagasikara soa.
Ny fitiavanay anaotsy miala,
Fa ho anao, ho anao doria tokoa.

Chorus:
Tahionao ry Zanahary
Ty Nosin-drazanay ity
Hiadana sy ho finaritra
He sambatra tokoa izahay.

Ry Tanindrazanay malala ô!
Irinay mba hanompoan'anao
Ny tena sy fo fanahy anananay,
'Zay sarobidy sy mendrika tokoa.

Chorus

Ry Tanindrazanay malala ô!
Irinay mba hitahian'anao,
Ka Ilay Nahary 'zao ton tolo izao
No fototra ijoroan'ny satanao.

Chorus

English translation

Oh, Our beloved fatherland
Oh good Madagascar.
Our love for you will not leave,
For you, for you forever.

Chorus:
Bless you, oh Creator
This island of our ancestors
To live in peace and joy
Hey! We are truly blessed.

Oh our beloved fatherland!
We wish to serve you with
The body and heart, spirit that is ours,
You are precious and truly deserving.

Chorus

Oh our beloved fatherland!
We wish that you will be blessed,
So that the Creator of this world
Will be the foundation of your laws.

Chorus

The High Constitutional Court has nine members who serve six-year terms. Three of the members are appointed by the president, three by the legislature, and three by the Council of Magistrates, a group of legal advisers. The High Constitutional Court evaluates the constitution and determines whether law and treaties abide by it.

The Court of Appeals reviews cases handled in lower courts. Most cases in Madagascar are tried in regional or city tribunals.

A court building in Antananarivo

City of the Thousand

Some of Madagascar's most incredible history and culture can be found in Antananarivo, its capital city. The city was first built at the end of the sixteenth century by the Merina king Andrianjaka. He demanded that his palace be built at the highest point in the city so that he could watch the land in every direction. The city's name means "city of the thousand" and refers to the thousand warriors that were said to have protected the palace hundreds of years ago.

Tana, as many locals call it, is the largest city on the island, with a population of 1,391,433 in 2016. It is the nation's cultural center, home to many schools, museums, and theaters. Located about 90 miles (145

km) from the east coast in the Central Highlands, the city is full of colorful wooden houses, as well as French colonial buildings. Major sites include the Queen's Palace and Andohalo Cathedral.

Cars and minibuses crowd the streets, sharing the room with motorcycles and ox-drawn carts. Modern office buildings butt up against rice paddies. Antananarivo is a beautiful city, but one that is fraying around the edges as time passes. Mixed in with the luxurious hotels and fancy shops is poverty, pollution, and a failing infrastructure.

Map: Antananarivo

0   0.25 mile
0   0.25 kilometer

FARAVOHITRA

Independence Plaza

Ambohitsorohitra Palace

Ambohijatovo Garden

Lake Anosy

Joseph Ravoahangy Andrianavalona Hospital

Andohalo Cathedral

St. Laurent Ambohimanoro Anglican Cathedral

Andohalo Garden

Mahamasina Municipal Stadium

Andafiavaratra Palace

Manjakamiadana

Antananarivo

Regional and Local Government

Madagascar is divided into twenty-two regions. The government in each region includes a governor and a regional council. Both the governor and the councillors are elected by the people. The regions are divided into districts that are in turn divided into communes. These groups also have elected councils and administrators.

Armed Forces

In Madagascar, the national defense is known as the People's Armed Forces. It combines the army, navy, air force, marines, and police into one group. Often the only way to tell the difference between the various parts of the armed forces is the hats people wear. The police wear blue hats known as *kepis*, and soldiers often wear red or black berets.

Soldiers march in a Madagascar independence day parade. About 13,500 people serve in the Madagascar military, and another 8,100 are in the national police force.

CHAPTER 6

Economic Struggles

WHILE MADAGASCAR REMAINS ONE OF THE most beautiful places in the world, it is also one of the poorest countries in the world. Studies have shown that the average Malagasy lives on less than $2 a day and that more than half of the population falls under the poverty level.

There are a number of reasons why this country is so poor. Past leaders have squandered money, spending it on luxuries when it should have gone to help the people. Because of the island's extreme isolation, it is expensive and challenging to conduct a lot of trade there. The weak infrastructure of Madagascar makes it impossible to reach many areas without the use of airplanes or boats. Without money to maintain roads, plus the damage from periodic cyclones and drought, travel is increasingly difficult. Farmers struggle to get their products to markets. Companies must spend a great deal of money getting

Opposite: **A farmer uses an ox to plow a rice field. People in Madagascar eat an average of about 240 pounds (110 kg) of rice per year.**

Until Madagascar achieved independence, the main type of currency used in the country was the French franc. Since 1961, the currency used on the island has been the ariary. Coins are available with values of $^1/_5$ ariary and $^2/_5$ ariary, as well as 1, 2, 4, 5, 10, 20, and 50 ariary.

The current banknotes used in Madagascar have values of 100, 200, 500, 1,000, 2,000, 5,000, and 10,000 ariary. Each bill also has the value in French francs in small numbers. The bills are quite colorful, featuring images representative of the island such as lemurs, zebu cattle, baobabs, rice fields, and fishers. In 2016, 3,222 ariary equaled US$1.00.

their goods across the ocean to other countries. Imports like food, machinery, and textiles cost far more to get than what is earned through the country's exports of coffee, vanilla, and sugarcane.

Ups and Downs

The economy is also affected by political events. During the six months in 2001 and 2002 when Ratsiraka and Ravalomanana argued over who had truly been elected president, trade between Madagascar and other countries almost came to a standstill. Tourism dropped more than 50 percent because visitors did not want to come to such an unstable country. Investors were not willing to invest their money in a place that seemed to be so volatile. It took years for the island to begin to recover from this period of political crisis.

There is hope for Madagascar's economy. Tourism is increasing again. People who are willing to put up with more primitive surroundings and simpler adventures are coming to the island. For them, having to travel across dirt trails filled with potholes to see what amazing animal or plant is waiting around the corner is worth it.

With the proper leadership as well as aid from foreign investors and grants from organizations, Madagascar may begin to thrive instead of just survive.

A Malagasy woman chops sugarcane, one of the nation's leading crops for export.

Working the Fields

Madagascar's economy is largely based on agriculture, followed by mining, fishing, and making clothes for export. Eighty percent of the island's workforce is involved in growing crops such as rice, cassava, sugarcane, cloves, and coffee. More than half of all the available land in Madagascar is used for rice paddies. Sugarcane is primarily grown in the south, while cassava, potatoes, corn, and yams are found in the Central Highlands. Bananas are a big crop on the east coast.

Madagascar is one of the world's leading producers of vanilla. Today, it produces about 3,100 metric tons a year, trailing only Indonesia. While many vanilla farmers once made a decent profit on their crops, many people are now using cheaper artificial vanilla. This has driven prices down and many vanilla farmers now struggle to survive.

Bananas are Madagascar's largest fruit crop.

Harvesting Vanilla Beans

Many delicious foods, from baked goods to ice cream, are flavored with vanilla. Have you ever thought where vanilla comes from?

Madagascar produces half of the world's vanilla. Most of it is grown in the northeastern part of the country.

Growing and harvesting vanilla beans is a very labor-intensive and slow job. Vanilla comes from a special type of orchid. It is a vinelike plant that grows up the side of a host or support tree. In Madagascar, each one of these plants has to be pollinated by hand. In pollination, the pollen seeds are transferred from the male plant to the female. This makes the female plant produce seeds. Without pollination, the vanilla orchid produces a flower but no seeds. The seeds come in a long pod, or bean. Six to nine months after pollination, the vanilla beans are ready to be harvested. This also

has to be done by hand, at the moment of peak ripeness. If the beans are harvested too soon, the flavor will be lost; too late, and the pods may start to split.

After the pods are picked, they are sorted by size, length, and appearance. They are cleaned and immersed in hot water for two to five minutes. Next, they are placed in a wooden box for forty-eight hours to "sweat" and turn brown. Then, they are spread out in the sun on racks and put back into the boxes to sweat some more, sometimes for several weeks. The beans smell wonderful by this time and have turned dark brown. Finally, the beans are placed on racks and left to dry for as long as a month. They are then tied into bundles and put in boxes for another two months. At last, it is time to ship the vanilla to other countries.

Zebu are particularly hardy cattle, able to tolerate high heat and humidity.

Minding the Herds

Land that isn't being used to grow crops in Madagascar is often used for raising cattle. The zebu cattle found throughout the island have a large hump on their backs and weigh hundreds of pounds. More than 19 million of them are scattered across the country. They are sometimes considered "walking bank accounts" since the more cattle a person has, the richer and more powerful he or she is.

In Madagascar, the zebu cattle are used for plowing and transportation. They are also used in religious ceremonies such as sacrifices, including at marriages, funerals, and holidays. The zebu provides food for a family. The people eat the meat and use the skin and fur for leather. Even the horns are put to use, used to make jewelry or cutlery.

In addition to raising cattle, the Malagasy also raise goats, pigs, chickens, geese, and turkeys. For those people who live on the coastlines, fishing is often the best way to earn money and put food on the table.

What Madagascar Grows, Makes, and Mines

AGRICULTURE (2013)

Rice	3,610,626 metric tons
Sugarcane	3,250,000 metric tons
Cattle	10,030,000 animals

MANUFACTURING (VALUE OF EXPORTS, 2014)

Metals	$667,000,000
Textiles	$625,000,000
Chemical products	$73,700,000

MINING (2012)

Ilmenite	660,000 metric tons
Tourmalines	48,000 kilograms
Sapphires	2,300 kilograms

Into the Forest

Although the amount of land in Madagascar that is covered in trees shrinks every single year, the forests still hold valuable trees, including ebony, rosewood, and sandalwood. These hardwoods are in high demand in other parts of the world and it is easy to understand why there is a drive to cut them down and sell them. However, doing this has worsened the island's problem of deforestation and made it harder for many animal species to survive.

Bricks are among the many products manufactured in Madagascar. At this factory, a worker lays out bricks to dry in the sun.

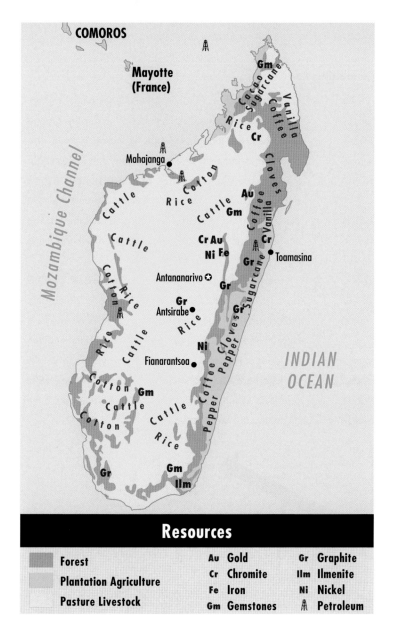

Resources

■ Forest	Au	Gold	Gr Graphite
■ Plantation Agriculture	Cr	Chromite	Ilm Ilmenite
□ Pasture Livestock	Fe	Iron	Ni Nickel
	Gm	Gemstones	⚒ Petroleum

Mining and Manufacturing

Madagascar is rich in gems and semiprecious stones. About half the sapphires unearthed in the world each year come from Madagascar. Tourmalines, garnets, and amethysts are also mined in Madagascar. In addition, the nation produces

For many years, the people living in the Melaky hills of western Madagascar had noticed a thick and sticky substance seeping out of cracks in the ground. They had no idea what it was and paid little attention to it, but others noticed it and wanted to capitalize on this newfound oil reserve.

Since two oil fields had been discovered in Madagascar in the early 1900s, several investors had been exploring the country for potential oil reserves. During the political unrest of the 1970s and 1980s, however, drilling slowed down. Lack of roads and reliable transportation made it unusually difficult to reach the richest oil reserves.

In 2009, when a political crisis brought the country to a halt, most of the gas and oil exploration stopped completely. That changed in 2014 when the island's government decided to offer much of its land to large companies, such as ExxonMobil and Chevron, for drilling.

While finding huge amounts of oil under the ground could help the island's delicate economy, it could also create environmental problems. Much of the oil is under the land used to raise herds of cattle. There is only a single river in the area with the most oil, and the river water would be needed to properly extract the oil. This could result in threats to the people and animals living in the area.

There is also concern that pipelines would be built close to the protected forest of Tsingy de Bemaraha. Biologist Steve Goodman says this area is diverse and unique. "If they build a pipeline, this would bring in different types of exploitation—companies would come to take the rare hardwoods and hunt the animals. If there were problems with the pipeline, it would be so terrible if the oil came out into this area."

ilmenite, which is the main ingredient in titanium, and mines iron, coal, nickel, and cobalt.

A variety of products are made in Madagascar. These include foods, clothing, soap, metals, bricks, and cement.

Services

Madagascar's amazing plant and animal life and unique history make it an increasingly popular site for tourists. Several hundred thousand people arrive each year to see the playful lemurs, the colorful birds, the towering rock formations, and the relaxed cities. The majority of them are from France.

France is also Madagascar's main trading partner. The country exports clothing, vanilla, cloves, fish, and other food products. It imports oil, chemical products, machinery, vehicles, and some food products.

Tourists photograph a leaf chameleon at a park near Antsiranana. Several hundred thousand visitors arrive in the country every year.

CHAPTER 7

The Malagasy

THE PEOPLE OF MADAGASCAR, COLLECTIVELY KNOWN as the Malagasy, are living in one of the poorest countries of the world, but they are friendly, hardworking, gracious, and, most of all, hopeful. They share whatever they have, believing in the Malagasy philosophy that "Even one grasshopper is to be shared."

Although their island began as the southern tip of Africa, most Malagasy do not consider themselves to be African. More than twenty ethnic groups are spread out over the island, and most people tend to identify with the distinct region they live in. Three-quarters of the population live in rural areas, while one-quarter lives in the city.

Opposite: **Malagasy children on Nosy Iranja inspect a crab.**

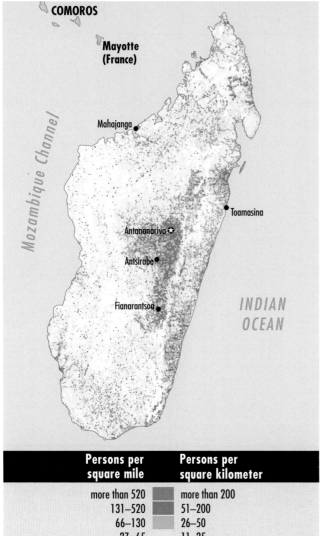

Persons per square mile	Persons per square kilometer
more than 520	more than 200
131–520	51–200
66–130	26–50
27–65	11–25
3–26	1–10
fewer than 3	fewer than 1

Population of Largest Cities (2016 est.)

Antananarivo	1,391,433
Toamasina	206,373
Antsirabe	186,253
Fianarantsoa	167,227
Mahajanga	154,657

The Island's Ethnic Groups

Madagascar's many ethnic groups emerged in different ways. Some have origins in old kingdoms. Some are based on regional identity. Some emerged as people who had a common way of making a living banded together.

The largest group of people in Madagascar is the Merina. Their name means "those from the country where one can see far." They make up one-quarter of the population and most of them live in the Central Highlands. The Merina are far more Asian than African in both their appearance and their culture.

The Betsimisaraka is the second-largest group and their name means "the many inseparables." They live on the island's eastern and northeastern coasts, which they share with the Anataloatra ("people of the sea"), the Antaimoro ("people of the shore"), the Antaifasy ("people of the sands"), and the Antanosy ("people of the island"). Many of these people raise rice, cassava, and corn, but have long been reputed as having been sailors and pirates.

The next largest group on the island is the Betsileo. Known

A group of Betsimisaraka people canoe in eastern Madagascar. They have long been known as sailors and fishers.

as "the many invincibles," this group is centered in the Central Highlands, especially around the capital city. They are known for their skill as rice farmers and wood-carvers.

The Sakalava are the "people of the long valleys." They live along the island's west coast and, of any of the Malagasy people, are the most similar in appearance to Africans. The Sakalava are known for raising zebu cattle. In the past they were also renowned for their seafaring skills and their ability to build and navigate outrigger canoes.

The Tsimihety people are found in the north-central region of Madagascar and are known as "those who do not cut their hair." They earned that name because in the early eighteenth century, their ancestors refused to cut their hair when a Sakalava ruler died, as was traditionally done as a sign of respect during mourning.

The Antaisaka people are found in the remote areas of the Tsaratanana Massif and southeastern coast of the island. They too are cattle herders and grow bananas, coffee, and rice. Many are fishers as well.

Ethnic Groups of Madagascar

Merina	26%
Betsimisaraka	15%
Betsileo	12%
Tsimihety	7%
Sakalava	6%
Antaisaka	5%
Antandroy	5%

A Few Missing Letters

The Malagasy alphabet is very much like the English alphabet, because of the first missionaries who came to the area hundreds of years ago. Over the years, the two alphabets have remained similar, except that the Malagasy do not use the letters c, q, u, w, or x.

Malagasy names are often very long and vowels like a and o are used repeatedly. Not all of the syllables in their names are pronounced, however.

Here is an example of Malagasy from Article 1 of the Universal Declaration of Human Rights. Notice the abundance of vowels throughout.

"Teraka afaka sy mitovy zo sy fahamendrehana ny olombelona rehetra. Samy manan-tsaina sy fieritreretana ka tokony hifampitondra ampirahalahiana."

In English, it is: "All human beings are born free and equal in dignity and rights. They are endowed with reason and conscience and should act towards one another in a spirit of brotherhood."

The Non-Malagasy Groups

There are four non-Malagasy minorities living in Madagascar: Comorans, French, Indo-Pakistanis, and Chinese. The biggest group among these is the Comorans, numbering about

A group of young Comorans relax at a mosque in Antsiranana.

A busy street in Ambalavao, in southern Madagascar

twenty-five thousand people. Their ancestors came from the Comoro Islands, which lie between Madagascar and Africa. Most Comorans are Muslim and live on the northern coast of Madagascar. Many work on the docks in the region, or in farm fields as laborers.

The French population is estimated to be about eighteen thousand people. Many work as military officers or business owners. About seventeen thousand Indo-Pakistanis known as *karana* in the Malagasy language, live in Madagascar. Most are Muslim and work as merchants along the island's west coast. The majority of the approximately nine

Common Malagasy Phrases

Salama	Hello
Salama tompoko	Hello, sir/madam
Misaotra	Thank you
Misaotra tompoko	Thank you, sir/madam
Azafady	Please/Excuse me
Veloma	Good-bye
Rano	water
Noana aho	I'm hungry
Mangetaheta aho	I'm thirsty
Vizako aho	I'm tired

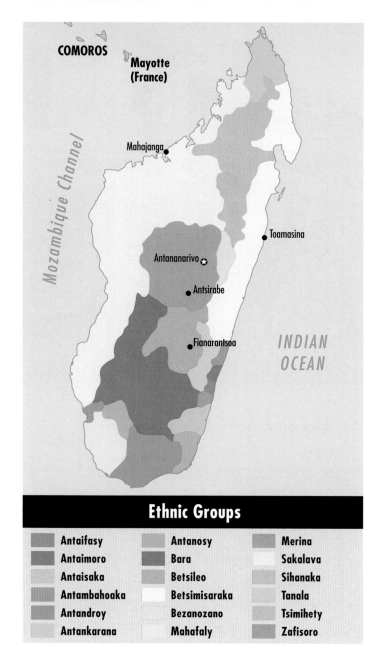

Ethnic Groups

Antaifasy	Antanosy	Merina
Antaimoro	Bara	Sakalava
Antaisaka	Betsileo	Sihanaka
Antambahoaka	Betsimisaraka	Tanala
Antandroy	Bezanozano	Tsimihety
Antankarana	Mahafaly	Zafisoro

thousand Chinese residents of Madagascar live on the east coast and in the capital city. Most work in trade.

A United Language

Although many different ethnic groups are scattered across Madagascar, they all speak the same basic language, known as Malagasy. This language is a combination of Indonesian, African, Arabic, and Malaysian. Some areas have different terms or slightly different dialects. For example, in the Central Highlands, *Manao ahoana* means "How are you?" But on the east coast, a person says *Akory* to ask the same question. In the north, "How are you?" is *Mbola tsara*, while in the southeast, it is *Salama*. No matter where a Malagasy travels, however, he or she is sure to be understood.

As a result of France being in control of Madagascar for so many years, French is still in use throughout the island, including in schools. French words are found in daily conversation and French terms are often used for ideas within science and technology. English is quickly becoming the third most common language in this country, as trade grows with other countries.

Body Language

Older people are always greeted first and with their appropriate title, Grandfather

Days of the Week and Numbers

Days of the Week	In Malagasy	Numbers	In Malagasy
Monday	alatsinainy	1	iray
Tuesday	talata	2	roa
Wednesday	alarobia	3	telo
Thursday	alakamisy	4	efatra
Friday	zoma	5	dimy
Saturday	asabotsy	6	enina
Sunday	alahady	7	fito
		8	valo
		9	sivy
		10	folo

Signs in Madagascar are often a mix of Malagasy and French.

The Malagasy **85**

or Mister, for example, as a sign of respect. This is traditionally followed by a handshake, using both hands. When greeting someone from afar, the Malagasy show respect by nodding, taking off their hats, and raising their right hands.

When saying no, a Malagasy shakes his or her head from left to right and says "*Ahn-ahn-ahn.*" The word *yes* is indicated with a nod and the statement "*Uhn-uhn.*" Close friends often walk hand in hand and sit very close to each other. When crossing between or in front of people, it is common to bend slightly or offer a quick apology.

Education

All children in Madagascar are required to attend school from ages six through fourteen. Primary school is free. In the

What's in a Name?

One of Madagascar's claims to fame is its long and complicated names. Cities, sites, and people almost always have names with twelve letters or more, and many are daunting for foreigners to try to pronounce. Imagine asking for directions to Antsohimbondrona or Tsiroanomandidy!

According to experts who have studied the Malagasy language, one of the reasons the names are so long is that each part of the name has a special meaning. In the past, the people of the island did not have separate first and last names. Instead, they were blended together, and sometimes even the region they came from or something about their heritage was inserted into the name.

For example:

Razafindranriatsimaniry = the grandson of the prince who envies no one

Andriantompokoindrindra = the prince who is my real lord

Translator Alain Rakotondrandria says that women who marry someone from their own region have the longest names among the Malagasy. The wives added their maiden names to their husband's names. In other words, if the single Miss Sahondra Lydia Rakotomalala married Mr. Andriatsiferanarivo, she would become Mrs. Sahondra Lydia Andriatsiferanarivo Rakotomalala.

nineteenth century, both Roman Catholic and Protestant missionaries set up missionary schools. Today, mission schools continue to educate many young Malagasy.

Education has improved greatly in recent decades. In the 1960s, less than 40 percent of Malagasy could read and write. Today, 65 percent of Malagasy are literate. The Central Highlands have higher literacy rates than the coastal regions.

Some Malagasy students continue on with secondary education and then go to a university. About forty thousand students attend universities in Madagascar, which include the University of Antananarivo, the University of Mahajanga, and the University of Fianarantsoa.

About half of primary school students in Madagascar are girls, but far fewer girls go on to secondary school.

CHAPTER 8

Blending Religions

MANY OF THE MALAGASY HAVE FOUND A WAY TO balance two very different religions: Christianity and their indigenous, or native, beliefs. More than half of the people on the island accept the idea of a single supreme god that they call Zanahary for "creator" or Andriamanitra for "sweet lord." At the same time, they also believe in *razana*, or the ongoing role of their dead ancestors.

According to Malagasy beliefs, there is a strong connection between the living and the dead. They believe that ancestors who are dead have the ability to affect the lives of the living,

Opposite: **Many people in Madagascar follow their traditional religion.**

A young girl takes Communion at a Roman Catholic service in Antananarivo. Nearly half the Christians in Madagascar are Catholic.

in particular a person's fortunes or misfortunes. For example, if ancestors are somehow offended by the words or behaviors of the living, they can cause trouble. Someone in the family might get sick or hurt. Crops might wither. Bad weather might come. Thus, it is essential that the living do all they can to make sure their dead relatives are remembered with honor and consulted for wisdom at all times.

The Tombs of Madagascar

Traditionally, in order to honor their ancestors, many Malagasy built elaborate and expensive tombs. Many of these burial sites cost more to build than people's houses did. Creating a beautiful tomb, however, remains one of the main ways the people of Madagascar can show respect to their relatives. Unknown dead, or those not remembered and honored, are thought to turn into *angatra*, or angry, evil ghosts bent on scaring and threatening people. Many islanders believe that a person's *ambiroa*, or soul, lives on inside the tomb, so it is considered essential that it be a place of peace and prestige.

Each ethnic group has its own style of tomb. The Merina, for example, traditionally built tombs of solid stone. Part of these tombs is underground, and inside is a chamber where bodies wrapped in silk shrouds are put on shelves. The Mahafaly and Antandroy create tombs from shaped rocks and then decorate

Mahafaly tombs often include statues and paintings.

Turning the Bones

The happiness of their ancestors is of such importance to the Merina people that two to seven years after people have been buried, their relatives bring the bodies back up. In a ceremony known as *famadihana*, or "the turning of the bones," the body is removed from the grave and wrapped in new, clean shrouds. The bones are handled by relatives, and then sprinkled with perfume or wine and washed. Often the family talks to the person as if he or she were still there. They may even get up and dance and sing with the bones. This ritual is considered an act of love. A traveler who happened to witness the famadihana stated, "I came expecting the most macabre of ceremonies, but instead found an extreme of adoration for loved ones that will forever change how I view life and death."

The turning of the bones is a celebration that can last up to a week. People come from all over the area to join the party, like a large family reunion. Feasts are prepared, music is played, stories are told, and then the body is returned to the grave. As the country has grown poorer, this tradition has begun to fade, because many families cannot afford to host such a large event.

the tomb with zebu horns and wood carvings known as *aloalo*. The Bara group bury their dead in the crevices of cliff sides. The wealthiest islanders might build tombs made of concrete and glass, while the poorest might just create simple cement tombs with a tin roof. What the tombs of all these groups have in common is that the outsides are often painted in bright colors and with images. In addition, there are sometimes statues on the tops of the buildings.

Consulting the Ombiasy

In order to better communicate with the dead, and to understand the messages they send, many of the Malagasy consult an *ombiasy*, a religious adviser and healer. It is the job of the ombiasy to consult the stars and understand *vintana*, or the fate of people based on the position on the moon, sun, and stars. Ombiasy are called on to decide exactly what day a house should be built or a couple should get married. They are asked to help figure out what to do when someone is ill or the weather is bad. Ombiasy are paid to make these predictions, and often use a combination of fruit seeds, corn grains, animal teeth, and glass beads to divine the answers.

Traditionally, the Betsileo people buried their dead in rock tombs.

In addition to helping families make big decisions and interpreting messages from the dead, the ombiasy also helps people to be aware of *fady*, or certain taboos (things that should

An ombiasy arranges seeds in an attempt to communicate with dead ancestors.

be avoided). Many of the fady are based on ancient folktales, while others are based on social values that are handed down from one generation to the next.

Taboos differ greatly from one ethnic group to another, and even from one village to the next. For example, there are a number of fady related to food. It is said that a person should never sing while eating, and in certain areas, should not whistle. It is forbidden to sit in the doorway of a house while the rice in nearby paddies is sprouting because the door of the house symbolizes birth. By blocking it, a person can stop the "birth" or growth of the rice. Because some people believe that evil spirits come out at night, all windows must be closed and doors locked when it gets dark. It is fady for the Sakalava people to eat pork or eel, or for the Antandroy to eat sea turtles.

Among some people in Madagascar, twins are taboo, or believed to be bad luck.

A Protestant minister leads a service in Madagascar.

The Role of Christianity

While the indigenous beliefs are strong in Madagascar, so is Christianity. Under the rule of King Radama I, British missionaries came to the island and converted many of the Malagasy. The missionaries published a Bible in the Malagasy language, and they opened religious schools and chapels. When Queen Ranavalona I came to power, she expelled the missionaries and banned Christianity. Anyone who didn't cooperate was executed. After her rule ended, Christianity returned, and today, it is the second most common religion on the island.

Some Christian leaders in Madagascar struggle to accept some traditional rituals, such as the turning of the bones. However, a growing number of them have acknowledged these traditions as part of the culture and work to find a way to support a belief in razana, while still worshipping and teaching about Zanahary.

Religious Holidays in Madagascar

March 29	Martyrs' Day/Memorial Day
March or April	Easter
May or June	Ascension Day
August 15	Assumption
November 1	All Saints' Day/Celebration of the Dead
December 25	Christmas Day

Children follow a man dressed as Santa Claus on Christmas Day.

CHAPTER 9

Creating and Playing

MADAGASCAR'S BEAUTIFUL SCENERY AND WILDLIFE often inspire art of all kinds. In Madagascar, the idea of beauty is often based on how practical or useful something is. An item that has been made from recycled materials is highly respected. The Malagasy people have been known to make oil lamps from discarded tin cans, eggs baskets from pieces of wire, and sandals from worn tires.

Wood-carving is a common form of art in Madagascar. In addition to making such useful things as stools and walking sticks, artists also sculpt figurines and other decorative items from wood and embellish them with intricately carved designs.

Opposite: **In Madagascar, tin cans are often used to make other goods, such as toy cars.**

As in many places, common proverbs in Madagascar hold clues about the culture's values and principles.

Among the Malagasy, almost every personal conversation or public speech contains at least one proverb. Here are a few:

"Truth is like sugarcane; even if you chew on it for a long time, it is still sweet."

"People are like plants in the wind; they bow down and rise up again."

"Like the chameleon, one eye on the future, one eye on the past."

"All who live under the sky are woven together like one big mat."

Art from the Loom

The women of Madagascar are known throughout Africa and around the world for the textile arts they make on looms. Using materials such as cotton, wool, silk, raffia and other plant fibers, plus a variety of natural dyes, they create everything from colorful pieces of clothing and burial shrouds to large tents or room dividers.

A weaver with her loom and silk

The Malagasy weave fine silk threads into cloth using a loom.

Malagasy weaving skills have been handed down from one generation to the next. "Our mother weaved, so I weave," says Madame Georgety, a member of a group of silk weavers in the Betsileo village of Soatanana." When we were young and would come home from school, we would weave." Women often use the same looms their grandmothers and great-grandmothers had used.

Making a silk cloth is neither a fast nor a simple process. First, wild silk cocoons from the forest must be found and gathered. Second, the silk is taken from the cocoons and put with other samples to be boiled and washed. Next, the silk is dried and spun by hand into thread. Dyes made from soil, flowers, berries, bark, leaves, and roots are added for color. Then finally the thread is put on the loom.

In 2004, the market for silk weaving was disappearing, but then the Peace Corps, a volunteer program run by the U.S. government, stepped in to help. A Peace Corps volunteer helped organize the silk weavers into a cooperative. Then she took their products and sold some in the island's larger cities and sent others back to the United States. Soon orders were coming in. In 2012, the story of the silk weavers' success was told in a documentary called *The Silkies of Madagascar*. "When [the

A woman shops for colorful cloth at a Malagasy market.

JEAN-JOSEPH RABEARIVELO

CET INCONNU ?

COLLOQUE INTERNATIONAL
DE L'UNIVERSITE DE MADAGASCAR

SUD

Caught Between Cultures

Jean-Joseph Rabéarivelo (1901–1937) is considered Madagascar's greatest writer. He was born in the city now called Antananarivo. As a teenager, his family lost everything when the French took control of the island. At thirteen, he began working as a proofreader, and soon he was writing poetry. Rabéarivelo felt torn between the two cultures of France and Madagascar, and his poems reflect that ambivalence.

Over the course of his life, Rabéarivelo wrote seven volumes of poetry. His poem "The Three Birds" shows his use of vivid symbolic language. It begins:

The bird of iron, the bird of steel
who slashed the morning clouds
and tried to gouge the stars
out beyond the day
is hiding as if ashamed
in an unreal cave.

weavers] make the lambas [cloth wraps] as part of the cooperative," explained a weaver named Madame Eugenie, "then there is enough money to buy food, there is enough money to buy medicine, there is enough money for school fees and for each family. So the life of each family is better."

Madagascar Music

The traditional music of Madagascar is different from that of most of Africa. Most African music relies heavily on drums and other percussion instruments. Traditional Malagasy music uses drums and rattles, but it also uses flutes, guitars, fiddles, and the *valiha*. The valiha is a stringed instrument made from

The valiha is considered the national instrument of Madagascar.

a hollow bamboo tube with at least twenty-one strings running down the length of the instrument. The musician plucks the strings to create sounds.

Modern music is heard throughout Madagascar. A style of music known as *salegy* has been popular since the late 1940s. It mixes the screech of electric guitars, the strong notes of accordions, and the pounding of drums. Played in nightclubs

Music from the Heart

One of the most popular musicians in Madagascar is Erick Manana. His career has lasted more than thirty years. Manana plays the acoustic guitar and sings. According to one reviewer, Manana "doesn't just sing his songs to the audience, it would be more fitting to say he lives them." Whether playing a traditional Malagasy ballad or his own version of a current pop tune, Manana thrills his audiences and keeps them coming back for more.

and parties, salegy includes a lead singer who calls out lyrics and other band members and dancers who respond. It is cheerful music, even though sometimes the lyrics reflect cultural problems.

Playing Ball

Soccer is the national sport in Madagascar, popular with people of all ages. Other popular sports include rugby, volleyball, basketball, boxing, and tennis. Madagascar has been competing in the Olympics since 1964. Athletes from the island have

Malagasy children play soccer anywhere they can find a little space.

When there are soccer games, the stadium in Antananarivo draws thousands of spectators.

participated in swimming, wrestling, judo, and weight lifting.

As a young boy growing up on the western coast of Madagascar, there was one important way to prove if you were tough and strong—a game of *moraingy*. This bare-fisted method of fighting was designed to test boys' strength and physical abilities, plus give them the chance to show off in front of others. Over the years, more and more people have played this sport and it has spread to other Indian Ocean islands.

A moraingy competition is held between two fighters, dressed only in shorts. Often the players are from different villages on the island. They circle each other and use their feet to kick as often as they use their fists to punch. The matches are one round, and only end when one of the players faints, falls down, gets hurts, or gives up. While they grapple, the audience cheers, yells, plays drums, or sings.

Moraingy fighting originated in the kingdom of Sakalava. It has now spread to regions beyond Madagascar.

A man hangs onto a zebu bull during a savika competition.

To be a hero in the Betsileo community, men have to do one thing: wrestle an angry bull. This Betsileo rite of passage, called *savika*, has been around for centuries. Boys who want to

A Winning Decathlete

One of Madagascar's most successful athletes is Kame Ali. Ali is a decathlete, meaning he has taken part in a decathlon, a ten-event sports competition. It consists of the 100-meter dash, long jump, shot put, high jump, 400-meter dash, pole vault, javelin, discus, 110-meter hurdles, and 1,500-meter run. In 2012, Ali won the Africa Decathlon Championship. In the years after, he continued to be one of the top decathletes in Africa.

prove that they are men, and single men who want to impress women, happily wrestle a zebu cattle, with its long horns and round hump. People also engage in this sport at some weddings and baptisms.

The first step in savika is getting the cattle angry, usually by poking and teasing it. Then competitors try to sneak up on the cattle and grab its hump and hang on as long as possible

Young men chase a bull around a ring during a savika rodeo.

Mancala can be played on a special carved board or by digging holes in the ground. Two players move around the board trying to capture each other's stones.

without getting trampled or injured. Savika is a dangerous sport, and there are no prizes for the winners, but they do earn the respect of the community.

Children's Games

The children of Madagascar spend much of their time helping

in the fields, watching over herds, and going to school. But they still find time to play. Two popular games are senet, an Egyptian game dating back to around 3500 BCE, and mancala, another ancient game.

Children often take part in clapping and singing games done in a circle with friends. And like other kids around the world, they enjoy friendly games of soccer, basketball, and volleyball. Malagasy children also enjoy sitting down together and sharing stories.

The National Game

Once upon a time, two brothers were vying to get their father's throne. The king was having trouble deciding which boy to pass it on to. One day, however, he felt ready to choose. He would pick his older son, Prince Andriantompokoindrindra. However, the prince was so fascinated with playing the *fanorona* board game that he could not stop. The king had no choice but to select the younger brother to be the next king.

Fanorona is Madagascar's national game, and it dates back centuries. Many people believe that the game symbolizes the idea that life is full of unexpected traps and pitfalls, as well as possibilities.

To play, two people sit opposite each other and control a set of either black or white pieces on a rectangular wooden board, much like chess. The goal is to capture as many of the opponent's pieces as possible or force them into a position where they can't move. Many children play the game using colored pieces of plastic, or rocks.

CHAPTER 10

A Malagasy Day

112

FOR MANY PEOPLE IN MADAGASCAR, LIFE LARGELY revolves around raising cattle and growing rice. Family is also important, from the youngest new members to the ancestors who have passed on but are still very much a part of everyone's lives.

Opposite: **A Malagasy man in western Madagascar**

Getting Married

In the past on Madagascar, parents often arranged marriages for their children. As time has passed, however, that tradition has been largely left

National Holidays

January 1	New Year's Day/Labor Day
March 29	Martyrs' Day/Memorial Day
March 30	International Women's Day
March or April	Easter
May or June	Ascension Day
May 25	Organization of African Unity
June 26	Independence Day
August 15	Assumption
November 1	All Saints' Day/Celebration of the Dead
December 25	Christmas Day
December 30	Anniversary of Second Republic

A young couple drives away after their wedding in Antananarivo. In Madagascar, men on average get married for the first time at age twenty-two and women at nineteen.

behind. Today, most young people make their own choice. The engagement process tends to vary from one ethnic group to another and is largely based on how traditional the family is. Typically, a man formally asks a woman's parents for permission to marry her. Both families may bring in a storyteller called a *mpikabary*. His role is to share the genealogy and history of each family so they know more about each other. A lamb is often sacrificed and zebu cattle are given to the bride's family. In more modern families, money is given instead of cattle.

The art of public speaking in Madagascar is often known as *kabary*. In the past, this style of talking was used to convey important information or tell legendary stories, but it has developed into a form of entertainment. Kabary can go on for hours. The skilled speaker is often called a *mpikabary*, and he may be called in to settle local disagreements or negotiate marriage dowries.

One of the key elements in this type of speech is that the speaker is expected to avoid using direct words. If he is speaking at a funeral, for example, his speech should never mention the deceased's name. Instead, he will rely on idioms and familiar phrases. The speech begins with an introduction and is followed by apologies to anyone the speech might offend or upset. Next are official greetings. Finally, there is a clear conclusion. Everything is said by memory, and often with a rhythm like that of poetry.

If the families are not sure the couple is a good match, they agree to a trial period of a year. If, within that time, either partner neglects his or her duties as a spouse, then the marriage is dissolved.

The marriage ceremony depends on an ethnic group's religion and traditions. Some ceremonies are very traditional, while others are based on Christian rituals. Wedding celebrations may last all day and into the night.

In the southern region of Madagascar, it is still relatively common to have more than one wife. Some men have three or four wives.

Divorce is common throughout the island. If a couple does end their marriage, it is traditional for the woman to keep all of the household belongings, while the man gets the house and custody of any children.

A doctor tends to a child in southern Madagascar. Child health in Madagascar has been getting steadily better. In 2005, fifty-one out of every one thousand children died before age one. By 2015, that number had dropped to thirty-three out of one thousand.

Welcoming Children

Family is very important to the Malagasy. Children are seen as gifts from God, and families have many children. The average family has seven children, but it is not unusual for people to have as many as thirteen.

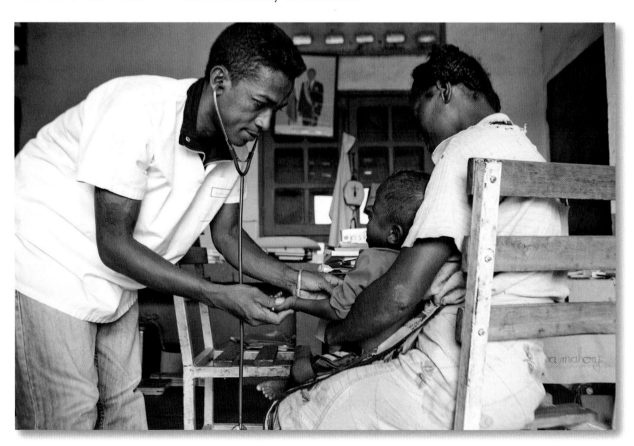

The Lamba

The clothing the people of Madagascar wear varies from one region to the next, but one of the most commonly worn pieces of clothing throughout the island is the *lamba*. The word means "cloth."

The lamba is traditionally woven from cotton or silk. It can be worn across one shoulder like a toga, or around both shoulders like a shawl. It is often added over skirts, shorts, or a long pair of pants. How a woman wears a lamba can indicate if she is single, married, or widowed. It can also indicate if someone is in mourning. Both women and men wear special ones for occasions like weddings or funerals. Women also use the wraps around their bodies for carrying their babies on their backs while walking or working. Additionally, when someone in Madagascar dies, the body is wrapped in a lamba before being put in a grave.

Lambas are sometimes exchanged between people of different regions as a sign of respect. In addition to being a versatile piece of clothing, these cloths are used as blankets, mats, pillows, or protection from the wind and sun.

Only the biggest cities have hospitals. Rural areas have to rely on the staff at health clinics or local, trained or traditional midwives when having babies. The first months of life are a dangerous time for infants, as they are vulnerable to disease. Out of every one thousand children born in Madagascar, thirty-three die before reaching the age of one.

A New Baby

Typically, newborns remain in the home with the family for the first seven days of their lives. There is often a special ceremony held the day the baby is brought out to meet the world. After that, babies are often carried on the mother's back, held in place by a *lamba*, or long piece of cloth tied around the woman's body. Other special ceremonies are held when a child is given the first haircut. This ritual is called the *ala volon-jaza*. Although the ceremony differs from one ethnic group to another, the cutting of hair is always celebrated as

A mother carries her baby on her back on a street in Ambalavao.

a sign that a child is joining the rest of society. Among the Antambahoaka group, in the southern region, the haircut is performed by the grandparents, while among the Merina, in the Central Highlands, the trim can be done only by a man whose parents are still living. The haircut is typically followed with a special meal. In some areas, coins are hidden in a bowl of rice and children try to find as many as they can.

From a very early age, Malagasy children are taught to help with household chores, including washing dishes, gathering water, watching cattle, working in the fields, and taking care of younger children.

A man carefully cuts a child's hair in Madagascar.

A Malagasy girl cooks rice over an open fire. In Madagascar, people eat rice with most meals.

Time to Eat

In Madagascar, mealtime usually means rice. It is the mainstay of every meal and every recipe. It might be in the main or side dish, or it might be the primary ingredient in a dessert. It is added to stews and combined with meat, beans, and vegetables. One of the most common dishes made in Madagascar is known as *ro*. It is a mixture of rice and herbs and leafy greens. *Romazava* is a broth made of green leafy vegetables with beef. A salad called *lasary* is sometimes eaten by those who like a little extra flavor. It is made from green mangoes or papayas. *Sakay* is a spicy condiment made from chili peppers, garlic, and ginger root. Coconuts are put to use also, especially in desserts.

Drinks are almost never served with meals, but instead are drunk separately. One of the most common beverages is *rano-vola*. This is made by boiling water in a pan where rice has just been cooked.

In rural areas, meals are typically eaten with everyone sitting on the floor. Almost all of the food served is hot; cold food

Madagascar dishes such as romazava, a soup shown here, use many vegetables.

is rare. Even desserts tend to be heated. Single plates are placed in the middle of the family group and each member reaches out with a spoon. The elders of the family are almost always allowed to eat first, as a sign of respect.

The protein served largely depends on where a family lives. Those on the coast tend to eat a great deal of fish and shellfish. In other places, people are more likely to eat beef or chicken.

It is very rare for the Malagasy to eat out, as that is usually reserved for the wealthy or for tourists.

Coconut Chicken

This recipe for *akoho sy voanio* contains some of the most popular ingredients throughout Madagascar: coconut and chicken. You can serve this alone, or over rice or noodles. Be sure to have an adult help you with this recipe.

Ingredients

1 whole chicken

2 tomatoes

2 onions

2 cloves garlic

4 teaspoons ginger

1 can unsweetened coconut milk

Oil, salt, pepper to taste

Directions

Sprinkle the chicken with salt and pepper. Slice the tomatoes into small cubes and set them aside. Add a small amount of oil to a frying pan. Sauté the chicken until done, over medium heat. Add onions to the pan. Continue stirring over medium heat until the onions are brown. Add garlic, ginger, and tomatoes to the pan. Sauté together briefly over medium heat. Add coconut milk and mix well. Reduce heat. Simmer over low heat for 30 minutes.

Serve with rice, noodles, or salad.

Koba is a popular sweet, often sold at markets and at stands on the street.

Favorite Snacks

Anyone visiting Madagascar is sure to be offered a taste of *koba*, the island's national snack. This snack is made of raw peanuts, brown and white sugar, rice, peanut oil, and water— all wrapped in a banana leaf and boiled. Vendors often stroll the streets of the island's largest cities with glass cases on their heads, containing all of koba's ingredients. They eagerly offer to make the dish for visitors.

Another popular snack or breakfast is called *mofo*. These are dough balls made from sweetened rice flour and flavored with banana, corn, or pumpkin. They can be eaten alone or with a meal.

Home Sweet Home

While the houses in Madagascar change from one region to the next, they all have one element in common: they are built out of locally available materials. Those materials often reflect how rich—or poor—a family is. For example, the families with more money might have walls made from wood, bricks, or concrete, while the poorer families rely on mud and brick to build their walls. On the coast, many homes are built on

Coastal houses are often raised to prevent them from flooding during storms.

Many Malagasy homes and businesses do not have electricity, so people use oil lamps to illuminate their late-night conversations.

raised platforms so that they are protected from damage when the rains, floods, and cyclones come each year. Common building materials include reeds, grasses, bamboo, and palm fronds because that is what is easily accessible. Coastal homes tend to be small, consisting of one to two rooms. Homes in the Central Highlands, on the other hand, tend to be much larger with two stories and even a balcony. In the northern region of the island, homes are generally made of red clay and tin roofs.

Most Malagasy homes will often have a sofa, chairs, and perhaps a few coffee tables. Walls are frequently covered with woven mats, posters, or calendars. Most homes do not have indoor bathrooms. Few have refrigerators, because electricity is scarce. Without electricity, families must rely on candles or kerosene lamps after it gets dark. Cooking is done over fires, as very few families have stoves.

Malagasy Hats

For many people, hats are a fun accessory to add to an outfit. For some of the people in Madagascar, hats are more than that. They are worn in order for a person to be respected. The Bara people often wear cone-shaped hats, while the Betsileo prefer four-cornered hats and the Merina wear hats made out of woven straw or rice.

Madagascar is a land filled with breathtaking beauty. Its isolation has made it possible for some of the world's most astounding creatures and wildlife to develop and thrive. This isolation has, however, also made it difficult for people to cope with a growing population and a shrinking number of resources. Despite these difficulties, the Malagasy people love their Island at the End of the Earth.

Forty percent of the people in Madagascar are under the age of fifteen.

Timeline

MADAGASCAR HISTORY		WORLD HISTORY	
		ca. 2500 BCE	The Egyptians build the pyramids and the Sphinx in Giza.
People arrive on the island of Madagascar.	ca. 2000 years ago	ca. 563 BCE	The Buddha is born in India.
		313 CE	The Roman emperor Constantine legalizes Christianity.
Arabs set up trading posts on the northwest coast.	600s CE	610	The Prophet Muhammad begins preaching a new religion called Islam.
		1054	The Eastern (Orthodox) and Western (Roman Catholic) Churches break apart.
		1095	The Crusades begin.
		1215	King John seals the Magna Carta.
		1300s	The Renaissance begins in Italy.
		1347	The plague sweeps through Europe.
		1453	Ottoman Turks capture Constantinople, conquering the Byzantine Empire.
		1492	Columbus arrives in North America.
Diogo Dias and his crew become the first Europeans to see Madagascar.	1500	1500s	Reformers break away from the Catholic Church, and Protestantism is born.
Dutch, French, Portuguese, and English arrive in Madagascar.	1500s–1600s		
		1776	The U.S. Declaration of Independence is signed.
		1789	The French Revolution begins.
Antananarivo becomes the capital of the Merina kingdom.	1800		
King Radama I makes a treaty with the British, solidifying Merina control of Madagascar.	1817		

MADAGASCAR HISTORY

British missionaries come to Madagascar.	**Mid-1800s**
The French seize control of Madagascar, making it a colony.	**1896**
France crushes an uprising by Malagasy fighting for independence, killing thousands.	**1947**
Madagascar becomes fully independent; Philibert Tsiranana is named president.	**1960**
Didier Ratsiraka is named president and rules for over 20 years.	**1975**
A new constitution is approved, establishing a democracy.	**1992**
The country's leadership is in limbo for six months following a disputed presidential election.	**2001–2002**
Cyclone Gafilo kills 237 people in Madagascar and causes devastating damage.	**2004**
Many people are killed during antigovernment demonstrations; President Marc Ravalomanana shuts down parliament.	**2009**
Madagascar is hit with a plague of locusts.	**2012**
Hery Rajaonarimampianina is elected president.	**2014**
Senate elections take place.	**2015**

WORLD HISTORY

1865	The American Civil War ends.
1879	The first practical lightbulb is invented.
1914	World War I begins.
1917	The Bolshevik Revolution brings communism to Russia.
1929	A worldwide economic depression begins.
1939	World War II begins.
1945	World War II ends.
1969	Humans land on the Moon.
1975	The Vietnam War ends.
1989	The Berlin Wall is torn down as communism crumbles in Eastern Europe.
1991	The Soviet Union breaks into separate states.
2001	Terrorists attack the World Trade Center in New York City and the Pentagon near Washington, D.C.
2004	A tsunami in the Indian Ocean destroys coastlines in Africa, India, and Southeast Asia.
2008	The United States elects its first African American president.

Fast Facts

Name of country: Republic of Madagascar

Capital: Antananarivo

Official languages: French, Malagasy

Antsirabe

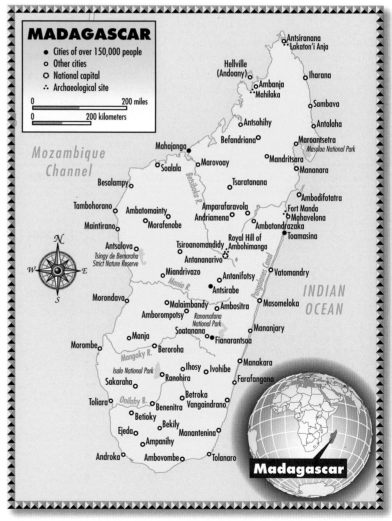

MADAGASCAR

- Cities of over 150,000 people
- Other cities
- National capital
- Archaeological site

200 miles
200 kilometers

Antsiranana
Lakaton'i Anja
Hellville (Andoany)
Iharana
Ambanja
Mahilaka
Sambava
Antsohihy
Antalaha
Befandriana
Maroantsetra
Masoala National Park
Mahajanga
Mandritsara
Soalala
Marovoay
Mananara
Besalampy
Tsaratanana
Mozambique Channel
Betsiboka R.
Ambodifotatra
Tambohorano
Amparafaravola
Fort Manda
Ambatomainty
Andriamena
Mahavelona
Maintirano
Morafenobe
Ambatondrazaka
Toamasina
Antsalova
Royal Hill of Ambohimanga
Tsingy de Bemaraha Strict Nature Reserve
Tsiroanomandidy
Antananarivo
Bongolanes Canal
Miandrivazo
Antanifotsy
Vatomandry
Mania R.
Morondava
Antsirabe
INDIAN OCEAN
Malaimbandy
Ambositra
Masomeloka
Amborompotsy
Ranomafana National Park
Manja
Soatanana
Mananjary
Morombe
Beroroha
Fianarantsoa
Mangoky R.
Isalo National Park
Ihosy
Ivohibe
Manakara
Sakaraha
Ranohira
Farafangana
Toliara
Betroka
Onilahy R.
Benenitra
Vangaindrano
Betioky
Bekily
Ejeda
Manantenina
Ampanihy
Androka
Ambovombe
Tolanaro

Madagascar

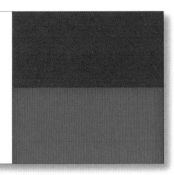

National flag

Tsingy de Bemaraha

Year of founding:	1960
National anthem:	"Ry Tanindrazanay malala ô!" ("Oh, Our Beloved Fatherland")
Type of government:	Republic
Head of state:	President
Head of government:	Prime Minister
Area of country:	226,658 square miles (587,041 sq km)
Latitude and longitude:	20°00' S, 47°00' E
Bordering countries:	None
Highest elevation:	Maromokotro, 9,436 feet (2,876 m)
Lowest elevation:	Sea level along the coast
Longest river:	Mangoky, 350 miles (563 km)
Largest lake:	Alaotra, approximately 900 square miles (2,300 sq km)
Highest recorded temperature:	97°F (36°C) in 1997
Lowest recorded temperature:	32°F (0°C) in 1932
Average annual precipitation:	39 to 59 inches (100 to 150 cm)

Fianarantsoa

Currency

National population (2016 est.): 25,060,196

Population of largest cities (2016 est.):

Antananarivo	1,391,433
Toamasina	206,373
Antsirabe	186,253
Fianarantsoa	167,227
Mahajanga	154,657

Landmarks:
- ▶ *Masoala National Park*, northeastern Madagascar
- ▶ *Nosy Boraha*
- ▶ *Ranomafana National Park*, southeastern Madagascar
- ▶ *Royal Hill of Ambohimanga*, Antananarivo
- ▶ *Tsingy de Bemaraha Strict Nature Reserve*, southern Madagascar

Economy: More than half of Madagascar's GOP comes from services. Just over a quarter comes from agriculture, including the production of coffee, vanilla, sugarcane, cloves, cocoa, and rice. The rest comes from industries such as food processing, and the production of goods such as soap and clothing. Madagascar is also a major producer of gemstones such as sapphires.

Currency: The Malagasy ariary. In 2016, 3,222 ariary equaled US$1.00.

System of weights and measures: Metric system

Literacy rate: 65%

Schoolchildren

Albert Rakoto Ratsimamanga

Common Malagasy words and phrases:

Salama	Hello
Misaotra	Thank you
Azafady	Please/Excuse me
Veloma	Good-bye
Aiza . . .	Where is . . .
Ohatrinona?	How much?

Prominent Malagasy:

Kame Ali (1984–)
Decathlete

Andrianampoinimerina (1745–1810)
Merina king

Erick Manana (1959–)
Musician

Jean-Joseph Rabéarivelo (1901–1937)
Poet

Gisèle Rabesahala (1929–2011)
Politician

Albert Rakoto Ratsimamanga (1907–2001)
Scientist

Philibert Tsiranana (1912–1978)
First president

To Find Out More

Books

► Dolan, Catherine. *My Madagascar*. Austin Macauley Publishers, Ltd. 2013.

► Frazel, Ellen. *Madagascar*. Bellwether Media, 2013.

► Gagne, Tammy. *We Visit Madagascar*. Mitchell Lane Publishers, 2013.

► Oluonye, Mary. *Madagascar*. Lerner Publications, 2013.

Movies

► *Island of Lemurs: Madagascar*. Warner Brothers, 2014.

► *Madagascar: The Land Where Evolution Ran Wild*. BBC, 2011.

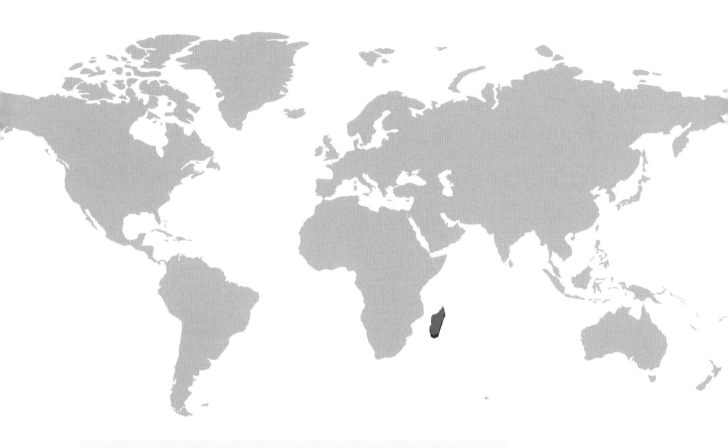

► Visit this Scholastic Web site for more information on Madagascar:
www.factsfornow.scholastic.com
Enter the keyword **Madagascar**

Index

Page numbers in *italics*
indicate illustrations.

Meet the Author

TAMRA ORR IS THE AUTHOR OF MORE THAN five hundred books for readers of all ages. She lives in the Pacific Northwest with her family, her cat, and her dog. She spends much of her time reading and writing. A graduate of Ball State University in Indiana, Orr loves to learn about places around the world and find out what makes each one unique.

Photo Credits